D0164366

Festivals

Ready, Steady, Play!

Series Editor: Sandy Green

Guaranteed fun for children and practitioners alike, the Ready Steady Play! series provides lively and stimulating activities
for children.

Each book focuses on one specific aspect of play offering clear and detailed guidance on how to plan and enjoy wonderful play experiences with minimum fuss and maximum success.

Each book in the Ready, Steady, Play! series includes advice on:

- How to prepare the children and the play space
- What equipment and materials are needed
- How much time is needed to prepare and carry out the activity
- How many staff required
- How to communicate with parents and colleagues

Ready, Steady Play! helps you to:

- Develop activities easily, using suggested guidelines
- Ensure that health and safety issues are taken into account
- Plan play that links to the early years curriculum
- Broaden your understanding of early years issues

Early years practitioners and students on early years courses and parents looking for simple, excellent ideas for creative play will love these books!

Other titles in the series

Books, Stories and Puppets 1-84312-148-4 Green
Construction 1-84312-098-4 Boyd
Creativity 1-84312-076-3 Green
Displays and Interest Tables 1-84312-267-7 Olpin
Food and Cooking 1-84312-100-X Green
Music and Singing 1-84312-276-6 Green
Nature, Living and Growing 1-84312-114-X Harper
Play Using Natural Materials 1-84312-099-2 Howe
Role Play 1-84312-147-6 Green

372.21
H49

Festivals

Carolyn Hewitson

Nyack College Library

David Fulton Publishers

David Fulton Publishers Ltd
The Chiswick Centre, 414 Chiswick High Road, London W4 5TF

www.fultonpublishers.co.uk

First published in Great Britain by David Fulton Publishers 2004

10 9 8 7 6 5 4 3 2 1

Note: The right of Carolyn Hewitson to be identified as the author of this work has been asserted by her in accordance with the Copyright, Designs and Patents Act 1988.

David Fulton Publishers is a division of Granada Learning Limited, part of ITV plc.

Copyright © Carolyn Hewitson 2004

British Library Cataloguing in Publication Data
A catalogue record for this book is available from the British Library.

ISBN 1-84312-101-8

The 'Photocopiable Materials' in this publication may be photocopied only for use within the purchasing organisation. Otherwise, all rights reserved. No part of this publication may be reproduced, stored in a retrieval system or transmitted, in any form or by any means, electronic, mechanical, photocopying or otherwise, without the prior permission of the publishers.

Typeset by FiSH Books, London
Printed and bound in Great Britain

#S6466019

Contents

Festivals

Welcome to *Festivals*, an exciting new publication which is part of the Ready, Steady, Play! series.

Get ready to enjoy a range of activities with your children, which will stimulate their all-round development.

The Ready, Steady, Play! books will help boost the confidence of new practitioners by providing informative and fun ideas to support planning and preparation. The series will also consolidate and extend learning for the more experienced practitioner. Attention is drawn to health and safety, and to the role of the adult.

How to use this book

Festivals is divided into two main sections, preceded by some general points to be considered by the reader.

The activity section encourages practitioners to help children explore festivals through both everyday activities and by introducing more unusual ideas. Each activity has an introductory page, providing background information to the festival and the practical aspect being addressed. Many activities also include follow-up material to support and extend learning.

The photocopiable section provides templates for the adult's convenience and rhymes, pictures and information for the children. These build on the learning aims of the set activities and are an ideal way of involving parents in their child's learning.

So read on, and enjoy... **Ready, Steady, Play!**

Sandy Green
Series editor

I was a reception teacher for twenty years and have been a supply teacher in several infant schools. Here are two quotes sum up what I feel about play and learning for the young child:

> Unlike other pedagogies that can be guilty of treating early infancy as a preparation for later childhood and adulthood and consequently seeing nursery education as a kind of ante chamber to later stages of formal education, the Reggio Approach considers early infancy to be a distinct developmental phase in which children demonstrate an extraordinary curiosity about the world.
>
> Marianne Valentine, *The Reggio Emilia Approach to Early Years Education*, The Scottish Consultative Council on the Curriculum, 1999

> I do not know what I may seem to the world, but, as to myself, I seem to have been only like a boy playing on the sea shore, and diverting myself in now and then finding a smoother pebble or a prettier shell than ordinary, whilst the great ocean of truth lay all undiscovered before me.
>
> Isaac Newton

Acknowledgements

Thank you to Alexander, Aman, Gethin, Jasmine Munjash, Joshua, Rizzi, Rhiannon and Zac; and to Avon Multicultural Centre (Chapter 2); Kulbinder Dio (photos Chapter 4), John and Gillian Beer for their Riddle poem from their anthology (Chapter 7); Toko Takahashi for the photographs, James Kirkup for his poem, and the Poetry Society (Chapter 9); Toko Takahashi for the photographs in Chapter 11; Enrico Arno's widow for the permission to use the 'Cricket' illustration, Myra Cohn Livingston for the poem 'First Thanksgiving', and Luckington Community School for the loan of a till (Chapter 16); Maria Salter for the speculaas recipe and loan of mould (Chapter 17); and for the kind permission by the Westonbirt National Arboretum Education Department, copyright – Ben Oliver for the Christmas Tree photographs (Chapter 18).

Series acknowledgement

The series editor would like to thank the children, parents and staff at:

The Nursery, Wadebridge Community Primary School, Wadebridge, Cornwall
Happy Days Day Nursery, Wadebridge, Cornwall
Snapdragons Nursery, Weston, Bath, Somerset
Snapdragons Nursery, Grosvenor, Bath, Somerset
Tadpoles Nursery, Combe Down, Bath, Somerset

for letting us take photographs of their excellent provision, resources and displays.

Also, John and Jake Green for their help throughout the series, and to Paul Isbell at David Fulton Publishers for his patience, enthusiasm and support.

Introduction

This is a practical handbook for Early Years students, practitioners and parents to help encourage understanding, awareness and enjoyment of some festivals celebrated in our multicultural society and throughout the world.

Hopefully the reader and children in his or her care will be tempted to discover more about the cultural and spiritual richness associated with these festivals. Positive, sensitive, tolerant and appreciative attitudes to a variety of beliefs and lifestyles can help young children feel confident in themselves and their relationships with others.

Some celebrations have an underlying religious significance, which is not relevant to very young children, but common themes such as food, presents, special clothes, stories and gathering together of families help affirm their own identities and encourage respect for those around them and those they may encounter throughout their lives.

Something to think about

It is important that practitioners show equal respect for all faiths and remember that some people have no religious faith, even though they take part in festivals. Some parents may wish to exercise their right to withdraw children from a particular celebration. For example Jehovah's Witnesses do not celebrate Christmas, Easter and birthdays, but have a service on the day of Jesus' death.

As human beings we share similar feelings about the journey of our lives, but it is important to remember that festivals are often part of a deeply held faith or national or cultural pride and identity, and should be respected as such.

Festivals should be respected for themselves and not manipulated to tick ELG boxes. They are unique, but similar in the way they try to answer the universal questions, which are: Who are we? and Why are we here?

Parents, grandparents, carers, friends and local communities are your best sources for finding out about festivals. It is very easy to get something wrong when interpreting a faith or festival, so rely on those sources to help you.

For checking the actual dates of festivals you could refer to *The Shap Calendar of Religious Festivals*, produced annually by the Shap Working Party and published by Hobsons.

For pictorial excellence I recommend *Celebration* in the Children Just Like Me series produced in association with UNICEF by Dorling Kindersley, 1997, and written by Barnabas and Anabel Kindersley.

Two other very helpful books are *Understanding World Religions in Early Years Practice* by Jennie Lindon, published by Hodder & Stoughton, 1999, and *Festivals Together: A Guide To Multi-Cultural Celebration* by Sue Fitzjohn, Minda Weston and Judy Large, published by Hawthorn Press, 1993, and reprinted 2003.

A catalogue that can supply multi-faith and multicultural material is available from The Festival Shop Ltd, 56 Poplar Road, Kings Heath, Birmingham B14 7AG; tel 0121 444 0444; email info@festivalshop.co.uk

Health and Safety

Throughout this book there are reminders about Health and Safety which I summarise:

- Check for allergies when tasting, eating and cooking.
- Make sure hands are clean.
- Some foods or substances can be irritants and cause eczema.
- Take care when cooking with knives, heat sources and pan handles.
- When doing creative work take care especially with scissors and small objects which can be swallowed or pushed up noses or in ears. Paint, crayons, felt tips, etc. must be safe for young children.

The adult role

A practitioner needs to be a facilitator and supporter for the activities in this handbook. Children need plenty of time to experiment and develop within safe boundaries.

Activities

The following pages contain 18 different activities suggesting a range of different ideas linked to festivals. Each activity follows a standard format to ensure ease of planning and implementation:

- the resources needed
- the aim(s)/concept(s)
- the process
- group size
- health and safety
- discussion ideas/language
- extension ideas
- links to the Foundation Stage Curriculum.

Key to Foundation Stage Curriculum abbreviations:

SS Stepping Stones

ELG Early Learning Goals

PSE Personal, social and emotional development

CLL Communication, language and literacy

MD Mathematical development

KUW Knowledge and understanding of the world

PD Physical development

CD Creative development

1 New Year

Introduction

The word January comes from Janus, the name of a Roman god who had two faces, one that looked forward and one that looked back. So at the same time he remembered the Old Year and looked forward to the New.

New Year is celebrated all over the world. The timing depends on the calendar you use, but common themes are shared. It is a time for a fresh start and new resolutions. It is a time to pay debts, and for sharing special food with family and friends and perhaps giving presents. Special traditions are observed and stories told.

The lunar year consists of 12 lunar months and is about 354 days long, so each year the dates of festivals based on a lunar calendar move back about 11 days in the solar calendar.

Chinese New Year is celebrated according to the Chinese lunar calendar and the date changes every year between 21 January and 20 February (see p. 5).

Al-Hijra is New Year's Day for Muslims and commemorates the journey made by the Prophet Muhammad from Mecca to Medina; the Muslim calendar is lunar, and Al-Hijra is celebrated in March (see p. 65).

Divali, a Sikh and Hindu festival, is celebrated in October or November (see p. 58).

Ethiopian Rastafarian New Year is on 11 September (see p. 46).

ACTIVITY 1

Making a calendar

Make a calendar as a book or a timeline.

Resources

- You need 12 large sheets of sugar paper or card with the names of the months of the year. You could use four different appropriate colours for the four seasons, e.g. green for spring.
- If you wish to make a timeline rather than a conventional calendar you will need the paper so it can be folded in half over a piece of string, ribbon or rope.
- Paper for children to draw themselves, which can be stuck on the calendar or timeline.
- Crayons, pencils, felt tips, scissors, spatulas and a table.

Aim/concept

- To begin to understand the pattern of time and the names of months of the year. To look back and forward and think about special days. To begin to be aware of different seasons.

Process

Explain to the children what you want them to do.

- Children draw pictures of themselves, and the practitioner or child cuts out.
- Each child glues the picture to the appropriate page (month) of his or her birthday.

Discussion/language

- Talk about special days such as Christmas and New Year
- Talk about the seasons, the weather, dark evenings, falling leaves
- Festival
- Celebrate
- Remember
- Looking forward
- Excitement
- Special food, clothes, candles, friends and family, presents

Group size

Whole group for discussion
Four to six for activity

Extension links

1. You may wish to begin the calendar in September at the beginning of the school year.
2. The practitioner looks at other recent festivals, which children in the group may have been celebrating or one the group is going to learn about.
3. Listen to and talk about the poem 'January brings the snow', see photocopiable p. 84.
4. Story poem *Chicken Soup with Rice: A Book of Months* by Maurice Sendak, published by Collins, 1964, sixth impression 1988.

Links to Foundation Stage

PSE	SS	Use talk to connect ideas, explain what is happening and anticipate what might happen next.
	ELG	Use talk to organise, sequence and clarify thinking, ideas, feelings and events.
	ELG	Listen with enjoyment, and respond to . . . poems.
CD	SS	Begin to use representation as a means of communication.
	ELG	Express and communicate their ideas, thoughts and feelings by using a widening range of materials.

Health and Safety

⚠ Care with scissors and glue

N.B. In some cultures children do not celebrate their birthdays and might not know when they are.

2 Chinese New Year

Introduction

Chinese New Year is celebrated by Chinese and Vietnamese communities all round the world. It looks forward to spring and marks the beginning of the Chinese lunar year (see p. 1). Once the festival lasted for 15 days, but now it is for 3, somewhere between mid-January and mid-February. It can be a religious or secular occasion. Houses are spring-cleaned, new clothes are bought and all debts are paid. Families get together for special meals and good fortune is hoped for in the New Year. In the streets there are lion dances, fireworks and dragon processions. Children are given red packets called Lai See. Good luck messages are written in gold and the packets contain money.

Background

A very long time ago in China the years had no names, so everyone got in a muddle and couldn't remember when they were born. The people went to the gods and asked them to solve the problem. The gods said, 'Why don't you give the years the names of animals?'

Twelve animals were chosen, but which name should come first? All the animals said why they thought they were the most important:

The tiger said he was the most handsome.

The ox or water buffalo said he was strongest.

The horse said he was fastest and the most useful.

The cockerel said he could wake people up.

The dragon said he was the fiercest.

The monkey said he was the cleverest.

The ram or sheep said his fleece kept people warm.

The hare or rabbit said he ran the fastest.

The boar or pig said he was the slowest!

The dog said he helped people and was their friend.

The snake said he was the most beautiful and graceful.

The rat didn't say anything, but he was thinking hard!

The gods decided that there should be a race across the river. The animals all lined up on the bank and jumped in.

They swam and swam and the ox was the strongest swimmer and was just about to step on the bank, when the rat, who had been sitting on the ox's back, jumped onto the bank. All the animals said he had cheated, but the gods said he had won.

This is how they finished:

1. Rat
2. Ox
3. Tiger
4. Hare
5. Dragon
6. Snake
7. Horse
8. Ram
9. Monkey
10. Cockerel
11. Dog
12. Pig

2004 is the year of the monkey

2005 is the year of the cockerel

2006 is the year of the dog

2007 is the year of the pig

2008 is the year of the rat

2009 is the year of the ox

2010 is the year of the tiger

See p. 91 for a photocopiable version of this picture – 'Chinese New Year calendar'.

ACTIVITY 2 Chinese New Year group drama

The New Year legend can be used for a group drama. When using any story to create a play, which encourages group participation, it is helpful to take a Pied Piper approach. The practitioner moves and tells the story, so if they wish, all children can take all parts. If the children are capable they can take turns being the gods and the animals.

Resources

- You will need pictures of the animals (see photocopiable p. 92)
- The story in your head or on paper (see p. 5)
- A long piece of cloth or paper for the river
- If you wish, paper plates and thin elastic or ribbon to make animal masks
- Crayons or felt tips for colouring
- Wool, fur, feathers, material, shiny paper
- Glue and spatulas

Aims/concepts

- To begin to understand and enjoy a Chinese festival
- To take part in imaginative role play
- To follow the sequence of a story
- To cooperate with others
- To gain confidence

Process

- Tell the Chinese New Year story.
- After discussion try moving like the animals, making their noises, then using masks if you wish, be the Pied Piper and lead the children through the story.
- If making masks, give each child a paper plate to colour.
- The practitioner will probably cut out eyes, nose and mouth.
- Children can stick on wool, bits of fur, material for the animals' coats or feathers for the cockerel or shiny paper for the snake.

Discussion/language

- Names of the animals. What do they look like?
- How do they move?
- Can they swim?
- What noises will they make?
- Which animal would you like to be?

Group size

Whole group for drama
Four to six for mask-making

Extension links

1. Find China on a globe or map.
2. Eat some Chinese food, prawn crackers don't need cooking!
3. Draw some Chinese characters, Chinese writing. You can use black paint and a brush or buy a Chinese ink pad and brush from an art shop (see 'Chinese writing', p. 10).
4. *The Story about Ping* by Marjorie Flack and Kurt Wiese, published by Bodley Head in 1935, is now in its 16th impression. It tells of a way of life on the Yangtze river in China which is fast disappearing, as economics and the damming of the river bring great changes.
5. *Once There Were No Pandas: A Chinese Legend*, by Margaret Greaves, illustrated by Beverley Gooding, published by Methuen, 1985.

For more information on Chinese New Year go to www.chinatownchinese.com

Links to Foundation Stage

PSE **SS** Have an awareness of, and show interest and enjoyment in, cultural and religious differences.

ELG Understand that people have different needs, views, cultures and beliefs, that need to be treated with respect.
Understand that they can expect others to treat their needs, views, cultures and beliefs with respect.

CLL **SS** Use talk to connect ideas, explain what is happening, anticipate what might happen next.

ELG Use language to imagine and recreate roles and experiences.

CD **SS** Play cooperatively as part of a group to act out a narrative.

ELG Use their imagination in art and design, music, dance, imaginative and role play, and stories.

Health and Safety

⚠ Some children do not like to wear masks and some find them frightening to look at.

⚠ Take care with glue and elastic.

Chinese writing

© Carolyn Hewitson (2004) *Festivals*, published by David Fulton Publishers Ltd.

3 No Ruz

Introduction

This takes place on 21 March and is New Year's Day for the followers of Zoroastrianism, an ancient Persian, monotheistic religion. Persia is now Iran. A week before the festival begins, spring-cleaning takes place. When the sun crosses the equator the New Year begins. Families dress in new clothes and eat a special meal, each member has a lighted candle and children are given toys, money, jewellery and a plant. If possible on the table is a goldfish in a bowl, and as the cannon goes off to signal New Year the fish is supposed to turn over in the water to symbolise the change of year, and everyone says, 'May your New Year be blessed.'

The largest group of Zoroastrians or Parsees, meaning 'Persian', live around Bombay in India, and migration has brought about a worldwide diaspora (movement to live in other countries).

ACTIVITY

3 Goldfish

To observe and look after a goldfish. Perhaps a child has one already.

To make a picture of a goldfish individually and make a class display.

Resources

- A goldfish
- An aquarium, tank or bowl
- Feed
- Pondweed
- A steady table
- Cut-out goldfish shapes (see photocopiable p. 93)
- Paint, crayons or felt tips
- Tissue paper or crêpe paper in various green colours

Aim/concept

- To begin to learn about a New Year or spring festival. To think about similarities with other festivals and learn about its uniqueness. To observe and find out more about a goldfish and caring for it.

Process

- Tell what happens at No Ruz.
- Have a goldfish, preferably in a tank not a bowl, with weed planted in gravel, water at room temperature, in daylight, but not strong sunlight. A group of children might help you setting it up. Have feed ready and read instructions to the children.
- Let groups of children observe and care for the goldfish.
- The practitioner can cut out the shape of a goldfish for each child (see photocopiable 'Goldfish', p. 93).
- Children can use a template shape or create a goldfish by drawing, painting or using collage.
- Paint or colour the goldfish while observing it.
- If you want a class display make a large tank shape in card or paper, let the children tear weed shapes from the tissue or crêpe paper and glue these onto the tank and let the children place their fish weaving in and out of the weed.

Discussion/language

- What do you and your family like to do at festivals or special days? Talk about food, clothes, presents and decorations and a well-cleaned house. Do family and friends visit?
- Talk about candles and a goldfish as important decorations for No Ruz.
- Does anyone keep fish? Where do they live? How do they breathe and what do they eat? How do you keep them clean?
- Aquariums.
- Gills and scales.
- Oxygen.
- How do they move?
- Do they jump or turn over?

Group size

Whole group for discussion
4–6 for activity

Links to Foundation Stage

KUW SS Examine living things to find out more about them.

ELG Find out about and identify some features of living things.

Extension links

1. The film *The White Balloon* recorded by PolyGram video is from Tehran. It is about a seven-year-old girl who wants to buy a goldfish for New Year.
2. Use a map or globe to find Iran and India.
3. Widen discussion to include caring for pets.

Health and Safety

⚠ A safe and solid base will be needed for a glass tank and water.
⚠ Make sure the goldfish is safe!
⚠ Take care with scissors and glue.
⚠ Crêpe paper if chewed or sucked stains faces and mouths!

4 Baisakhi

(can be spelt Vaisakhi)

Introduction and background

Sikhs and Hindus celebrate Baisakhi on 13 April, as the first day of the New Year. Baisakhi is also the day when Guru (holy teacher) Gobind Singh called all Sikhs to meet together because, although Sikhs were peace-loving, they were being attacked for their beliefs. Five brave men showed they would die for their faith if necessary. The Guru gave these men the name a Singh (lion) and from then all male Sikhs are called Singh and females Kaur (princess).

Sikhs all over the world celebrate for three days, reading from scripture, praying and singing at the Gurdwara or place of worship. Vegetarian food is prepared and served by everyone in the *Langar* or hall. Everyone, not just Sikhs, is welcome to enter the Gurdwara and eat in the *Langar*. Men and women share the responsibilities in the *Langar*. Guru Gobind Singh established the *Khalsa*, the Sikh community, and the five symbols of Sikhism.

These are:

A *Kirpan* – a dagger showing willingness to fight, but only in self-defence.

A *Kara* – a steel band worn on the wrist to remember all Sikhs are joined in unity.

Kesh – uncut hair, a gift of God. Men cover their hair with a turban.

A *Kangha* – a comb to keep hair in place.

Kachera – cotton shorts worn for freedom of movement to fight to defend the faith.

Clothes

What do we know about clothes?

What can we find out about clothes with special reference to traditional Punjabi Sikh clothes?

Resources

- Clothes that children are wearing when the activity begins.
- Any special purpose, special occasion clothes they are allowed to bring.
- Dressing-up clothes already in the Early Years setting and any borrowed from home.
- Pictures of traditional Punjabi Sikh clothes, e.g. a turban, shalwaar kameez.
- Punjabi Sikh clothes to try on; this may not be possible.
- If possible some clothes from a variety of cultures to try on.
- See photocopiable pages on:
  - 'How to put on a sari', p. 94
  - 'How to put on a turban', p. 95
  - 'Shalwaar Kameez', p. 96
- Look at pictures of children round the world in different clothes.
- See book list (p. 107).

Aims/concepts

- To find out how weather, culture, occasion, identification and comfort affect what we wear.
- To begin to be able to dress and undress independently.

Process

- Talk about the festival Baisakhi.
- Talk about some of the reasons why we dress as we do.
- Think about the names of clothes we wear for specific activities, e.g. pyjamas, swimsuits, etc.
- Look at the way our clothes fasten.
- Encourage bringing special clothes from home.
- Look at pictures of children from around the world. Barnabas and Anabel Kindersley's *Celebration*, in the Children Just Like Me series from Dorling Kindersley in association with UNICEF, is excellent.

Discussion/language

- Baisakhi
- Singh, lion
- Kaur, princess
- Guru
- Gurdwara
- Shalwaar kameez
- Sari
- Turban
- Wool, cotton, silk, leather
- Warm, cold, wet, dry
- Velcro, laces, zip, buttons, hooks, toggles
- Pyjamas, tracksuits, jeans
- Uniform – nurses, police officers, soldiers, fire fighters
- Trainers, wellies, sandals, slippers, boots
- Bracelets, earrings, necklace, rings

- What do we wear when it is hot, cold, wet, etc.?
    – when we go to bed?
    – when we play games?
- Why do we need to recognise uniforms?
- How do we fasten our clothes?
- Can we dress ourselves?
- What are our favourite clothes?

Links to Foundation Stage

PSE **SS** Have an awareness of, and show interest and enjoyment in, cultural and religious differences.

ELG Understand that people have different needs, views, cultures and beliefs that need to be treated with respect.

KUW **SS** Explore objects.
Show an interest in why things happen and how they work.
Sort objects by function.

ELG Look closely at similarities, differences.
Ask questions about why things happen and how things work.

Extension links

1. See Divali, another Sikh festival (p. 58). At Divali Sikhs celebrate the release from prison of Guru Har Gobind, who was imprisoned for refusing to give up the Sikh faith. He would only agree to being released if Hindu prisoners were also released.
2. Sorting clothes by type, material, fastening, etc.
3. Use catalogues for pictures of clothes for sorting.
4. You can buy wooden fabric-printing blocks from ethnic craft shops and use them for paint printing on paper or material to create Indian fabric patterns. I have bought blocks showing patterns of elephants (see below).

- For paint mix see 'Harvest', p. 54.
- The Galt catalogue for early learners has authentic multicultural dressing-up clothes, puppets and dolls.

Stories about clothes

- *Old Hat, New Hat* by Stan and Jan Berenstain, Collins Picture Lions, 1973.
- 'The Emperor's New Clothes', traditional.
- *How Do I Put It On?* by Shigeo Watanabe, Bodley Head, 1979.
- 'O Soldier, Soldier Won't You Marry Me?' traditional song.
- 'The Three Little Kittens', traditional.

5 Oranges and Lemons Day

Introduction and background

On the last day of March at the church of St Clement Dane in east London, children attend a service and receive presents of fruit.

After a long winter with little fresh fruit, except, maybe, some stored apples, in medieval times in northern Europe people would be happy to see the arrival of barges carrying fruit from the Mediterranean to the wharves just below St Clement Dane. Porters, who carried the fruit to Clare Market, were charged a toll to cross the property of Clement's Inn. St Clement Dane's bells ring 'Oranges and Lemons'. The bells tolled as prisoners were led to public execution, so we have 'Here comes a chopper to chop off your head.'

ACTIVITY 5 Finding out about Oranges and Lemons

Sing the nursery rhyme 'Oranges and Lemons' and play the game.

How to play Oranges and Lemons

Two children are chosen. One is the Orange team leader the other the Lemon. All sing 'Oranges and Lemons'.

The two chosen children make an arch and the other children skip round under the arch in single file. Children making the arch make a chopping movement with their arms at 'Here comes a chopper'. When 'the last man is dead' is reached, the child under the arch is caught and chooses to be an Orange or Lemon and holds on around the team leader's waist and the game and song start again and go on until no one is left. Traditionally there is a tug-of-war between the two teams. Probably best left out!

For copies of the rhyme, see the photocopiable 'Oranges and Lemons nursery rhyme', p. 97.

Taste and possibly use oranges and lemons for cooking.

Resources

- Oranges and lemons – a group of 4–6 children need 2–3 oranges and lemons
- Table
- Knife
- Squeezer
- Jug
- Beakers
- Paper roll
- Aprons

Aims/concepts

- To enjoy singing and playing a nursery rhyme, with which the children are probably familiar.
- To begin to understand a link with the past and a festival.
- To learn about healthy eating.

Process

- Sing 'Oranges and Lemons' – use a tape if necessary.
- Play the 'Oranges and Lemons' game.
- Hold, feel, smell, describe oranges and lemons.
- The practitioner cuts the fruit horizontally.
- Children look at the fruit and describe the inside and lick fingers.
- Squeeze the fruit.
- Taste the juice.

Discussion/language

- Oranges and lemons
- Juice
- Pips and seeds
- Skin and pith
- Segments
- Do children know how they taste?
  - sweet
  - sour
- Fruit keeps you healthy. Which fruits do you like to eat?
  - Where do they grow?
  - Do they grow on trees?
- Barges and wharves
- Mediterranean
- Markets
- Church bells

Group size

Whole group for singing and playing (not all children may want to join in)
Four to six for tasting

Links to Foundation Stage

KUD **SS** Describe simple features of objects and events.

ELG Investigate objects and materials by using all of their senses as appropriate.

CD **SS** Begin to build a repertoire of songs.

ELG Sing simple songs from memory...match movement to music.

Extension links

1. Fruit printing, see 'Harvest', p. 54.
2. Cookery: make orange and lemon biscuits, see cookery book or photocopiable 'Orange and Lemons biscuit recipe', p. 93.
3. Pancakes for Shrove Tuesday, see p. 26.
4. Find the Mediterranean on a globe or map. How would the boats get to England and London?

Health and Safety

⚠ Allergies
⚠ Clean hands
⚠ Aprons
⚠ Take care with the knife
⚠ Children with skin problems such as eczema may need to wear disposable gloves.

6 Lent, Shrove Tuesday and Carnival

Introduction

Lent is a 40-day period before Easter. Some Christians fast or give up things they like in memory of Jesus' fast in the desert. See the New Testament, St Matthew, Chapter 4. Many Christians used to give up eating meat. The word carnival comes from the Latin *carne vale* or goodbye to meat. Shrove Tuesday is the day before Lent when eggs and butter needed to be used up before the Lenten fast.

A few days before Lent there are carnivals in many parts of the world – Brazil in South America, Trinidad in the Caribbean, and Venice in Italy. There are parades, and people wear fancy dress and masks, and dance and sing and make music.

ACTIVITY

6 Pancakes

Make and eat pancakes

Listen to a pancake poem

Poem for pancakes, see the photocopiable 'Pancake poem', p. 99

Resources

- A table
- Aprons
- Recipe for pancakes, see the photocopiable 'Pancake recipe', p. 26

Ingredients

- Eggs
- Flour
- Milk
- Water
- Butter
- Sugar
- Lemon juice

Equipment

- Medium mixing bowl
- Large mixing bowl
- Measuring jug
- Sieve
- Weighing scales
- Rubber or plastic spatula
- Whisk (electric or hand)
- Tablespoon measure
- Pancake pan
- Pan to melt butter in
- Lemon squeezer
- Cooker
- Plates
- Spoons
- Forks
- Napkins

Aim/concept

- To enjoy cooking and eating a traditional food which is associated with Shrove Tuesday. To begin to understand the background to Lent and Carnival.

Process

- You may wish to tell the story of Jesus' fasting in the wilderness and talk about fasting in the Muslim religion (see Ramadan, p. 64).
- Make and eat pancakes (see recipe, p. 26).
- Listen to pancake poem (photocopiable p. 99).

Discussion/language

- Carnival, *carne vale*
- *Mardi gras*, fat Tuesday or Shrove Tuesday
- Lent
- Ramadan
- Has anyone or their family fasted?
- Have children eaten pancakes?
- Sweet or savoury
- Have children seen the Olney pancake race on television?
- Has anyone been to a carnival, seen floats, and heard steel bands?
- Cooking words
- Heavier, lighter, more, less
- Whisk
- Measure
- Melt
- Sieve
- Toss
- Sizzle

Questions

- Why do we need a recipe?
- Why do we measure?
- How do we melt butter?
- Where do the ingredients come from? E.g. milk from cows.
- Remember to talk about change, the melting butter, the ingredients mixing together, the wetness of the mixture and the dryness of the pancake.

Group size

Whole group for background and introduction and the poem
Four for cooking

Links to Foundation Stage

CLL	SS	Question why things happen, and give explanations.
	ELG	Sustain attentive listening, responding to what they have heard by relevant comments, questions…
MD	SS	Order two items by weight or capacity.
	ELG	Use language such as 'greater', 'smaller', 'heavier' or 'lighter' to compare quantities.
KUW	SS	Show an awareness of change.
	ELG	Ask questions about why things happen and how things work.

Extension links

1. To 'Oranges and Lemons Day', p. 19
2. To 'Easter' exploring eggs, p. 28

Health and Safety

- ⚠ Clean hands
- ⚠ Take care with source of cooking heat, electric whisk
- ⚠ Food allergies
- ⚠ Oil splashes

Pancake recipe

Makes 12–14.

110g plain flour
Pinch of salt
2 large eggs
200ml milk and 75ml water mixed together
2 tablespoons melted butter
Alittle extra butter for cooking the pancakes
Lemon juice
Caster sugar

Sieve flour and salt onto a large mixing bowl.

Break 2 eggs into the flour.

Whisk eggs into flour and begin to add a little of the milk and water mix.

Whisk until the batter is smooth, like thin cream. The mixture can be used straightaway.

When you are ready, add the 2 tablespoons of melted butter to batter and stir in.

Melt about a teaspoonful of butter in the pan and swirl it round to grease the whole pan.

The pan needs to be greased, but any excess butter should be tipped onto a saucer. Get the pan really hot then turn heat to medium and pour in 2 tablespoons of batter.

Tip the pan to coat it evenly with batter; it takes about half a minute to cook.

If the pancake is thin it will be cooked through, and unless you are feeling confident there is no need to toss it. Try it once, just for fun!

Make sure the pan is greased each time you make a pancake.

Slip the pancake onto a warm plate.

Have squeezed lemon juice and caster sugar ready to sprinkle on; fold it in half and in half again to form triangles.

Allow children to help as much as they are able.

© Carolyn Hewitson (2004) *Festivals*, published by David Fulton Publishers Ltd.

7 Easter

Introduction

Around 21 March many northern countries celebrate festivals related to spring time and the end of winter. Before food was easily available all year round, people had to rely on various forms of preservation and hoped there would be enough to last through the winter until new food could be grown and animals born.

The word Easter comes from the name Eostre the Saxon goddess of spring. Easter's date varies, because it is kept in relation to the Jewish Passover, which changes with phases of the moon. The Christian festival celebrates the resurrection of Jesus Christ after his death by crucifixion on Good Friday.

Spring, Easter, resurrection and eggs are all associated with new life. Eostre has a hare as a sacred companion. In many European countries children prepare nests, and decorate or search for hidden eggs brought by the hare or Easter Bunny.

Egg exploration followed by hard-boiled egg decoration.

Resources

- Eggs for observation
- Hard-boiled eggs for decoration
- Egg cups
- Aprons
- Paper towels
- Whisk
- Bowl
- Felt tips
- Table

Aims/concepts

- Close observation of eggs
- To learn more about eggs

Process

- Feel and describe eggs.
- Crack and name parts.
- Separate.
- Whisk.
- Decide if cooking should follow this activity. You don't want to waste the eggs. I suggest pancakes, omelette, scrambled egg or meringues.
- Have hard-boiled eggs ready or boil them so children can watch.
- Decorate the hard-boiled eggs, using felt tips, with faces or patterns.
- Put them in egg cups and make a display; they can be eaten later.

Discussion/language

- Where do eggs come from?
- What may they develop into?
- Shells – hard, brown, white, speckled
- How do they roll?
- What do you think is inside?
- White, yolk, yellow, slimy, slippery, fluffy
- Uses
- Poached
- Scrambled
- Fried
- Boiled
- Omelette
- Cakes and biscuits
- Meringues
- Custard

Group size

Four to six

Extension links

1. Talk about other egg layers, e.g. alligators, turtles and dinosaurs.
2. Stories about eggs:
   – *Flap Your Wings* by P. D. Eastman, A Collins Early Bird, 1969.
   – *The Very Hungry Caterpillar* by Eric Carle, Hamish Hamilton, 1970.

A riddle

A box without hinges, key, or lid,
Yet golden treasure inside is hid.

(Answer: an egg)
From the *Delights and Warnings* poems selected by John and Gillian Beer, published by Macdonald.

Links to Foundation Stage

KUW **SS** Examine objects and living things to find out more about them.

ELG Investigate objects and materials by using all their senses as appropriate.

SS Show an awareness of change.

ELG Ask questions about why things happen and how things work.

Health and Safety

⚠ Clean hands
⚠ Take care if cooking or boiling
⚠ Any allergies?

8 Passover or Pesach

Introduction

This is a Jewish festival celebrated in late March or early April.

Passover is the Jewish festival of freedom celebrating the Jewish people's escape or Exodus from slavery in Egypt. The stories of Moses and the bulrushes and of the Exodus can be found in the Old Testament in the book of Exodus, Chapters 2 and 12, telling the origin of the festival of Passover, and Chapters 13, 14 and 15.

Background

When the people of Israel first came to live in Egypt they lived and worked as free people. A new Pharaoh came to power and made the Jewish people slaves. Moses was saved from death when, as a baby, he was placed in a basket to float on the River Nile and was found by Pharaoh's daughter. He grew up to be the leader of the Jewish people. Many times Moses asked Pharaoh to let his people go, but not until God had sent many plagues, such as fleas, sickness and darkness, did Pharaoh say yes.

The Jewish people were in such a hurry to leave they didn't have time to let their bread rise, so they baked it unleavened. Pharaoh changed his mind, but the waters of the Red Sea parted, the Jewish people were saved, and the Egyptian soldiers drowned.

Festival

This is an eight-day festival, which begins with spring-cleaning. On the evening before Passover children search the house for pieces of hametz or ordinary bread, which their mother has hidden. No leavened bread is allowed at Passover time, to remember the flight from Egypt, when there was no time for the bread to rise.

The food eaten at the Seder meal (Seder means order) on the evening of Passover symbolises the Passover story. Two of the foods served are Charoset and Matzos. The mixture symbolises mortar, which glued together the bricks used in the building in Egypt, which the Jewish people were forced to do as slaves. Matzos are unleavened bread, symbolising the bread which was taken by the Jewish people as they escaped from Egypt, and which had no time to rise.

Passover story and food

Tell the Passover story and eat some of the traditional Seder food.

Resources

- The story of baby Moses (see 'Background')
- The story of the Jewish people's freedom from slavery
- Charoset (pronounced Haroset, the H being made as a guttural sound in the back of the throat)
- Apple, walnuts, sugar, cinnamon and grape juice
- A bowl, grater, knife and spoon
- Aprons
- Small bowls and spoons for children
- A packet of Matzos found in most supermarkets with the cheese biscuits
- A white napkin
- Table, chairs
- Paper roll

Aims/concepts

- To begin to understand and enjoy a Jewish festival.
- To follow the sequence of a story.
- To begin to understand the conventions of eating together, one of the common themes in the celebration of festivals.
- To try new tastes.

Process

- Tell the story of Moses and the origins of Passover.
- Traditionally, on Passover eve, the youngest child in the family asks the family, 'Wherefore is this night different from all other nights?' And then the Passover story is told.

To serve the Passover Seder meal

- To make Charoset, see the photocopiable 'Charoset recipe', p. 100.
- Let the children wrap the Matzos in a napkin and share out the pieces. Let them share the Charoset, then pour the grape juice to drink. Let the children sit round the table and enjoy sharing and eating and tasting together.

Discussion/language

- Moses
- Egypt
- Pharaoh
- Jewish people
- Slaves
- Freedom
- Plagues
- Exodus

- Seder meal
- Pesach or Passover
- Matzos – compare this with risen bread. Perhaps the children have baked bread?
- Charoset
- Mortar
- Eldest, youngest

Talk about special meals, rituals, food and table settings children have experienced, e.g. Christmas or birthday parties. (Some children may not have experienced sitting at a table.)

Group size

The whole group, if this story is told separately.
Four to eight children for the Seder meal with one or two practitioners.

Links to Foundation Stage

PSE	SS	Have a sense of self as a member of different communities.
	ELG	Have a developing respect for their own cultures and beliefs and those of other people.
MD	SS	Count up to three or four objects by saying one number and name for each item.
	ELG	Use developing mathematical ideas and methods to solve practical problems.
KUW	SS	Describe significant events for family or friends.
	ELG	Begin to know about their own cultures and beliefs and those of other people.

Extension links

1. Hanukkah, another Jewish festival.
2. Sukkot, another Jewish festival.

Health and Safety

⚠ Take care with the chopping knife or grater.
⚠ Remember food allergies, especially walnuts.

9 Hina Maturi or Japanese Dolls' Day

雛 祭 り
(HINA MATU RI)

Introduction

This traditional Japanese celebration held on 3 March is for girls and is sometimes called a March or peach festival. It has its origins in an ancient Japanese Shinto religious festival of ritual purification. Paper dolls called *hitogata* are placed on rivers or streams, and as they float away, impurity, bad luck or bad health disappear.

Most Japanese girls have a set of dolls too precious to play with, which are displayed in the best room of the house on a red-tiered stand. The Emperor and Empress are displayed on the topmost tier, on the second level the court ladies, and on the third sit five musician dolls. Furniture, tableware, a mandarin tree and cherry blossom are provided for the dolls.

The tiered stands of dolls may be displayed before 3 March, but as soon as this date arrives, everything is put away. It is believed that if the dolls are displayed indefinitely, a girl's chance of marriage may be delayed.

Girls under 14 years are considered too young to make the display, and so mothers do it for them.

Talking about something precious

Talk about the dolls' festival.

Read the poem, 'The doll festival' by James Kirkup, see photocopiable p. 101.

Look at photos of Japanese dolls.

Talk about things that are precious to us and encourage children to bring a precious doll, toy or object for display.

Resources

- Shelves covered in red paper suitable for display
- Dolls, ornaments, objects and toys brought by children
- Poem, 'The doll festival', photocopiable p. 101
- Map or globe
- Any interesting objects available from Japan

Aims/concepts

- To begin to understand and enjoy a Japanese festival.
- To talk about precious and favourite things from home.

Process

- Talk about the Dolls' Day celebration. Boys' Day is celebrated on 5 May (see p. 43).
- Look at and talk about the photographs and any other Japanese objects available.
- Talk about making a display of precious things from home.
- Decide how and where to put the display. (Parents and carers will need to know about this.)
- Make a display, altering positions from time to time.
- Talk about what the children have brought and how they look after them.

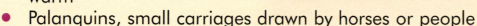

Discussion/language

- Where is Japan on a map or globe?
- Emperor and Empress
- Gauze, silk, brocades
- Samisen players (Japanese guitar players)
- Bonsai, a tiny tree
- Braziers, heaters for keeping people and food warm
- Palanquins, small carriages drawn by horses or people
- Kimono
- Precious
- How can we take care of people and things precious to us?
- Position on shelves – top, middle, bottom
- Higher or lower, bigger, smaller
- Imagine the Emperor and Empress come to life and what they might do with the other people and objects on the shelves.

Group size

Whole group for discussion and showing what they're going to display.
Four to six for arranging and rearranging the display.

Extension links

1. Try some Japanese picture-writing.
2. See p. 87 equipment for Chinese picture-writing.
3. See Japanese Boys' Day, p. 43.

Stories about dolls

- *The Little Girl and the Tiny Doll* by Edward and Aingelda Ardizzone, A Young Puffin published in 1979 and reprinted many times.
- *Buy Me a China Doll* by Harve Zemach, illustrated by Margot Zemach, published by Blackie, 1969. Adapted from a delightful, funny, cumulative Ozark song from Missouri, USA.

Stories about things which are precious

- *Sarah's Room* by Doris Orgel, pictures by Maurice Sendak, Bodley Head, 1972.

Health and Safety

⚠ Make sure the display is positioned so the display and the children are safe.

Links to Foundation Stage

CLL	SS	Use vocabulary focused on objects and people who are of particular importance to them.
		Extend vocabulary, especially by grouping and naming.
	ELG	Extend their vocabulary, exploring the meanings and sounds of new words.
MD	SS	Observe and use positional language.
		Use size language such as 'big' and 'little'.
	ELG	Use everyday words to describe position.
KUW	SS	Gain an awareness of the cultures and beliefs of others.
	ELG	Begin to know about their own cultures and beliefs and those of other people.

10 Wesak

Introduction

This takes place in May or June according to the lunar calendar.

This is the most important Buddhist festival, because it celebrates the birth, enlightenment and death of Buddha on one day. Buddhists decorate their homes and shrines with candles, lanterns and flowers. In Thailand and Sri Lanka, where there are many Buddhists, beautifully decorated elephants take part in processions.

Buddhists do not worship Buddha as a god, but try to follow the example of the Buddha's life and teachings.

Background

When the Buddha was young he was called Siddhartha, and the following story tells of his special love for all living creatures. His cousin Devadatta liked to hunt, and when a swan flew overhead he shot it with his bow and arrow. When the swan fell to the ground, Siddhartha found it first and gently removed the arrow from its wing. He took good care of the swan and stopped the bleeding by pressing leaves on the wound.

The boys argued, saying the swan belonged to each of them. They asked some wise men who was right. They said the one who saved the swan could care for it. Siddhartha nursed it and set it free. Many caged birds are set free at Wesak.

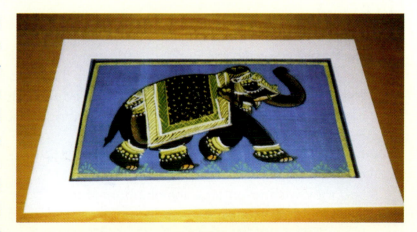

ACTIVITY 10 Making decorated elephants

Tell the story of Siddhartha and the swan.

Make a display showing a procession of decorated elephants in collage.

Resources

- Copy of the story
- Map or globe
- Elephant shapes cut out of card, enough for each group
- Paint, glue, spatulas, scissors
- Brightly coloured material, sequins, ribbons for making and decorating the elephants' costumes
- Felt tips for decorating the trunks and heads of the elephants
- Table
- Paper for collage background

Aims/concepts

- To begin to know about other cultures and beliefs and to think about caring for animals.
- To enjoy and listen to a story.
- To experiment with colour and texture to make a collage.
- To cooperate with others.

Process

- Tell the story of Siddhartha and the swan.
- Explain he is called the Buddha and people worldwide try to follow his example.
- Talk about caring for people and animals (N.B. No Ruz, p. 11).
- Talk about elephants being especially loved in parts of the world and the work they do, e.g. carrying people and heavy things. They help to celebrate the Buddha's special day.
- Use the photocopiable elephant shape (p. 102) ; use grey paint or paper and decorate.
- You may wish to enlarge the elephant shape.
- The elephant usually wears a large piece of decorated material over its back like a large saddle, and the trunk and around the eyes are decorated with special paint.

Discussion/language

- How do we care for people we know, and how do they care for us?
- How do we care for animals we have as pets?
- Can we understand our own and others' needs?
- Food
- Shelter
- Warmth
- Safety
- Love
- Friends
- Family
- Freedom
- Siddhartha
- Buddha
- Procession
- Decorate
- Thailand and Sri Lanka (N.B. see Divali, p. 58)
- Find Thailand and Sri Lanka on a map

Group size

Whole group for discussion and story
Four to six for making collage

Links to Foundation Stage

PSE	SS	Show care and concern for others, for living things and the environment.
	ELG	Consider the consequences of their words and actions for themselves and others.
KUW	SS	Gain an awareness of cultures and beliefs of others.
	ELG	Begin to know about their own culture and beliefs and those of other people.
CD	SS	Use ideas involving fitting, overlapping. Choose particular colours to use for a purpose. Work creatively on a large or small scale.
	ELG	Explore colour, texture, shape, form in two dimensions.

Extension links

Stories about elephants

- *The Elephant and the Bad Baby* by Elfrida Vipont and Raymond Briggs, published by Picture Puffin, 1971.
- *The Blind Men and the Elephant* by John Godfrey Saxe and Paul Galdone, published by World's Work; this is a traditional Indian legend and there are many versions.
- *Elmer: The Story of a Patchwork Elephant* by David McKee, published by Dobson, 1968.
- 'The Elephant's Child', a wonderfully funny story from *Just So Stories* by Rudyard Kipling, published by Macmillan; there are many editions.
- See p. 18, 'Baisakhi', for using printing blocks to make elephant patterns.

Health and Safety

⚠ Take care with scissors, glue and especially small sequins.

Japanese Boys' Day or Children's Day

Introduction

Originally this was a festival for boys, but now it is celebrated as Children's Day. It is a national holiday. Parents hope their boys will grow strong, brave and healthy just like the warrior Samurai dolls which families display on tiered shelves. Samurai were courageous Japanese warriors and the dolls are for display only. Parents hope all their children will grow up healthy.

Japanese irises, *shobu*, are put into a boy's bathwater. This custom is known as *shobo-yu*. The word for a contest shares the same pronunciation as the word for iris, *shobu*. Hopefully these boys will grow up to win all the contests in life.

Outside houses where there are boys, carp banners and streamers are attached to a long bamboo pole and blow in the wind.

The carp, or *koi* in Japanese, is a strong, brave fish, which can leap a waterfall and swim against the current.

Carp banner

To talk about Japanese Children's Day

To make a carp banner

Resources

- Picture of a carp, if possible
- See 'Carp template', photocopiable p. 103
- Card
- Red, blue, black, white, yellow and orange tissue paper
- Glue and spatulas
- Scissors
- Table
- Thick sewing thread

Aim/concept

- To begin to understand and enjoy a Japanese festival, make a carp banner and talk about growing up brave and healthy, and good and kind.

Process

- Cut out a carp shape in card from photocopiable p. 103 or allow children to draw around template and cut out. Tear pieces of tissue paper for scales, eyes, gills and tails; make long streamer pieces for the tails.
- Stick on in patterns of colour.
- The practitioner can thread sewing thread through the mouth, and if it's a windy day the children can try flying their carp banners.

Discussion/language

- Samurai warriors
- Iris flowers
- Carp, fish and banners
- Scales, gills, fins and tails

- Talk about growing up healthy, brave, good and kind.

- What happens when the wind blows?

Group size

Whole group for discussion
Four to six for making carp banners

Links to Foundation Stage

PSE	SS	Have an awareness of the boundaries set and behavioural expectations within the setting.
	ELG	Understand what is right, what is wrong and why.
KUW	SS	Gain an awareness of the cultures and beliefs of others.
	ELG	Begin to know about their own cultures and beliefs and those of other people.
PD	SS	Show some understanding that good practices with regard to exercise, or eating, sleeping and hygiene can contribute to good health.
	ELG	Recognise the importance of keeping healthy and those things which contribute to this.
CD	SS	Make constructions, collage.
	ELG	Explore colour, texture, shape, form and space in two or three dimensions.

Extension links

- See Japanese Dolls' Festival, 3 March, p. 35.

One, two, three, four, five,
Once I caught a fish alive.
(Traditional nursery rhyme.)

- Try some Japanese food. Supermarkets sell sushi and noodles.
- Try using chopsticks. Remember food allergies.

Health and Safety

⚠ Care with glue and scissors
⚠ Food allergies

12 Haile Selassie Day

Introduction and background

Emperor Haile Selassie I was born on 23 July 1892. He became Emperor of Ethiopia in 1930. In 1935 Ethiopia was attacked and annexed by Mussolini and his Italian army. Haile Selassie and his court and family went into exile. When Ethiopia was freed by British forces in 1941 he returned and began to modernise the country. He was deposed in a military coup in 1974.

One of the oldest Christian churches in the world was established in Ethiopia, and Rastafarian beliefs are based on the Bible. Many Rastafarians live or originate from Jamaica and further back as slaves from Africa.

Marcus Garvey, a Jamaican born in 1887, was leader of the first Rastafarians, and believed to be the reincarnation of John the Baptist. He accepted Haile Selassie as the living God and hoped Rastafarians in the Caribbean and America would find a new pride in their African roots and heritage.

Some beliefs originate in the Old Testament. Rastafarians do not eat pork, shellfish or any fish over 18cm long. They do not cut their hair, as commanded in Leviticus, Chapter 21, Verse 5. Men twist their hair into dreadlocks – dread means respect – and cover their hair with a knitted tam. Women may wear a tam or a headscarf.

Coffee, milk and rum may not be drunk, only fruit juice; and food is not salted. Their diet is mainly vegetarian.

Rastafarians follow the Ethiopian calendar. It has 13 months in a year and begins on 11 September, when Rastafarians celebrate New Year. The years are named after the apostles Matthew, Mark, Luke and John in a four-year cycle. 2003 is named after Luke and so on.

JOHN	2004
MATTHEW	2005
MARK	2006
LUKE	2007
JOHN	2008
MATTHEW	2009

As in African culture, Rastafarian drumming is central to religious worship and celebration. The pitch and sounds of the drums follow those of African languages. There are three important drums: bass like thunder; fundie like an earthquake; repeater like lightning. From drumming and chanting came reggae and the music of Bob Marley.

ACTIVITY
12 Bang the drum

To learn something about being a Rastafarian

To make some simple drums and experiment with basic music ideas using these drums.

Resources

- A variety of containers such as cocoa tins, dried milk tins, tins without sharp edges; plastic containers such as yoghurt pots; pots and pans from the playhouse.
- Lids made from thick paper; silver foil using several layers; heavy-duty polythene.
- Rubber bands; ribbon; string; strong tape.
- Scissors.
- Simple drumsticks; dowelling or bamboo; a circle of material stuffed and held onto the stick with tape or a rubber band, or, of course, use fingers.
- The children will soon find ways of making their own drums!
- Map or globe.
- Tape or CD of reggae music, especially Bob Marley.

Aims/concepts

- To begin to understand a little about Rastafarianism.
- To enjoy listening to, dancing to and drumming with reggae music.

Process

- Find Ethiopia, Jamaica and the UK on the map.
- Talk about travelling to live in other countries.
- Listen to tape or CD.
- Try clapping the rhythm.
- Try moving to the beat.
- Try identifying the instruments.
- Let the children make their own drums.
- Show the children the resources you have collected and together make the drums.

- Experiment!
- This activity can be in a group with an adult or the drums can be left in a music corner for children to use when they wish.

N.B. Don't feel you need to achieve results. Children are experimenting and improvising. A simple list of ideas for these early experiences is found under 'Discussion/language', below.

Discussion/language

- Talk about travelling to other countries to live and work. Do the children know anyone who has done this?
- Africa, Ethiopia, Jamaica, UK.
- Reggae music. Can they give a name to other music?
- Pop, jazz, classical, film, TV songs they sing at school, home, church, mosque, temple, etc.
- Names of instruments they know.

Group size

Four

Extension links

1   Other musical instruments
2   Stringed instruments
3   A shoebox, no lid, with elastic stretched around the length
4   Rattles
5   Plastic bottles with dried peas or rice inside

There are many simple instruments from a wide variety of cultures available from education catalogues.

Health and Safety

⚠ Care with scissors and rubber bands

Links to Foundation Stage

PSED	SS	Show curiosity. Have a strong exploratory impulse. Have a positive approach to new experiences.
	ELG	Continue to be interested, excited and motivated to learn. Be confident to try new activities . . .
KUW	SS	Gain an awareness of the cultures and beliefs of others.
	ELG	Begin to know about their own cultures and beliefs and those of other people.
PD	SS	Respond to rhythm . . . by means of . . . movement.
	ELG	Move with confidence, imagination and safety.
CD	SS	Tap out simple repeated rhythms and make some up.
	ELG	Recognise and explore how sounds can be changed . . . recognise repeated sounds and sound patterns and match movements to music.

Stories and poems

Anancy stories originated in West Africa and were brought to the Caribbean by slaves. Ananse, Anansi or Anansy is a mythical, magical folk hero, who is both man and spider. According to legend he brought stories from the gods. During slavery, African people tried to preserve as much of their oral traditions, culture and language as they could. Anancy is Brer (brother) Rabbit in America and Brer Anancy in the Caribbean.

- There are many Anancy stories in print; one of my favourites is *A Story, A Story* by Gail E. Haley, first published in Britain by Methuen Children's Books, 1972.
- *The Leopard's Drum*, by Jessica Souhami, is an Asante tale from West Africa, published by Frances Lincoln, 1995, with stunning illustrations, colours and patterns.
- An excellent poetry collection is *A Caribbean Dozen*, edited by John Agard and Grace Nichols and published by Walker Books, 1996.

N.B. Orthodox Christians in Ethiopia celebrate Fassika or Easter, the day when Jesus rose from the dead.

Basic music ideas

- Variation in loudness – how to achieve it.
- Variation in speed – how to achieve it.
- Variation in texture – number of instruments, taking turns, all together, some then one, etc.
- Variation in tone – the sorts of sounds instruments make (this applies more if you follow this activity up by making and playing a variety of other instruments).
- Endings, beginnings, middles, repeat.
- The feeling that music creates, and how it is done.
- Using a steady beat.
- Using rhythms.

Discussion before starting is useful, but most often the ideas come as the children play.

Pieces of music do not need to have titles or stories or even a mood. Let the child decide.

13 Harvest

Introduction and background

Before we could buy most foods all year round at the supermarket, food for the winter months had to be harvested and preserved. Grain crops such as oats, wheat and barley were cut with half-moon shaped knives called scythes, then tied in bundles and left in the fields to dry. When they were dry they were threshed or beaten to separate the grain from the straw and chaff.

So, having successfully finished the hard work, and with plenty of food ready for winter, there was feasting and celebration. It was an ancient pre-Christian festival.

In Britain it used to be the custom on 1 August, Lammas Day, to take to church a loaf made from the first grain harvested, and the bread was used for holy communion.

ACTIVITY 13 Fruit and vegetable printing

Fruit and vegetable printing

Naming fruit and vegetables

Resources

- Paper which will absorb paint, e.g. sugar paper
- Paint
  - Paint either in the colour of the fruit and vegetables or limit colours if you want a pattern.
  - A little PVA glue mixed into the paint helps adhesion.
- Pieces of foam in foil or plastic containers
- Fruit, vegetables. I suggest peppers, apples, lemons, oranges, pears, potatoes and mushrooms, which print successfully.
- Table covered with newspaper
- Aprons
- Paper towels for wiping hands
- Knife

Aims/concepts

- To investigate fruit and vegetables
- To print and make patterns with fruit and vegetables

Process

- Name and talk about fruit and vegetables you are using.
- Practitioner, or children if they are able, cut fruit and vegetables in half horizontally.
- Drain fruit and vegetables by placing the cut side down on paper towels.
- Have paint mixed with a little glue ready in foil or plastic containers, or if children are able, let them do the preparation.
- Press cut side on foam or sponge.
- Press cut side on paper; repeat.
- Some children may be happy to do neat, regular printing, but for some it will be a new experience and they need to experiment.
- Some will use a piece of potato, e.g. to rub around on the paper until there is a hole in it; do not despair!

- Remember when you did something new for the first time and think how much background experience you have.
- Children need to find out about wet and dry, where to position things, what happens when . . .
- Perfection will come much later, so resist doing this for them.
- Encourage, praise and perhaps do some printing alongside them.
- You may find some children won't do this activity because their hands get messy, and others will try to eat the fruit and vegetables!

Discussion/language

- Names of fruit and vegetables used
- Colours of fruit and vegetables used
- Feel, smell and shape of fruit and vegetables – rough, smooth, round, etc.
- Which are fruit? Which are vegetables?
- Likes, dislikes
- Do we eat five pieces of fruit and vegetables a day?
- Cut in half-circles
- Segments – wheels, spokes
- Juicy, dry
- Pips, seeds

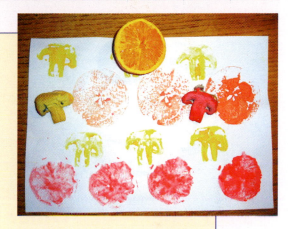

Group size

Naming and handling fruit and vegetables – whole group
Printing – four children

Extension links

1   Thanksgiving – fruit and vegetables in America, p. 71
2   'Oranges and Lemons' – fruit, p. 21
3   Pesach (Passover) – fruit, p. 32
4   Lent – lemons, p. 24
5   Thanksgiving – pumpkins, p. 76
6   St Nicholas Day – orange rind, p. 81
7   Ramadan, p. 64. Oranges and lemons originate in the Middle East.

Stories

- 'The Enormous Turnip', traditional.
- 'The Little Red Hen', traditional.
- *Avocado Baby* by John Burningham, Jonathan Cape.
- *Handa's Surprise* by Eileen Browne, Walker Books.
- *Mr Rabbit and the Lovely Present* by Charlotte Zolotow, illustrated by Maurice Sendak, HarperCollins Picture Lions.

Health and Safety

⚠ Allergies
⚠ Take care with knife
⚠ Clean hands

Links to Foundation Stage

MD   SS   Show awareness of symmetry.

ELG   Talk about, recognise and create simple patterns.

KUW   SS   Examine objects and living things to find out more about them.

ELG   Investigate objects and materials.

SS   Give time for exploratory play. . .

ELG   Give opportunities, some adult directed, some child initiated, to investigate, using a range of techniques and senses.

PD   SS   Show some understanding that good practices with regard to . . . eating . . . can contribute to good health.

ELG   Recognise the importance of keeping healthy and those things which contribute to this.

Other harvest festivals

- Sukkot is Jewish harvest festival during which little outside shelters are decorated with harvest fruit and vegetables.
- Thanksgiving is an American festival, literally giving thanks for the harvest, celebrated by some of the new settlers from Europe and their neighbours the North American Indians (see p. 71).

Other activities

- Try tasting some fruit and vegetables, 'Try tasting fruit & veg.', p. 57
- Baking bread
- Growing pips and seeds
- Using seeds inside plastic bottles to make shakers

Try tasting fruit & veg.

Some ideas for tempting children to try tasting fruit and vegetables

N.B. Allergies

Vegetables

Celery – chop the stalks and fill the curve with cream cheese.

Baby carrots peeled and eaten raw.

Red, yellow and orange peppers chopped very small and eaten raw.

Tiny peas used for counting and popped in the mouth one by one.

Sweetcorn boiled or steamed whole, the kernels dipped in melted butter.

Raw vegetables dipped in hummus.

Baked potatoes made into hedgehogs by sticking chopped sticks of celery or carrot in between cut edges.

Faces made with vegetables. Cucumber slices for eyes, red pepper strips for lips and a carrot baton for a nose and sticking-up hair.

Do include some fruit and vegetables the children may not have tried, e.g. avocado, pomegranate and passion fruit.

© Carolyn Hewitson (2004) *Festivals*, published by David Fulton Publishers Ltd.

Divali

Introduction

This is a festival celebrated by Hindus and Sikhs. Divali means a row of lights and it is interpreted in various ways in different parts of India and the world where Indians live. It marks the beginning of the Indian financial year.

Hindus may pray to Lakshmi, the goddess of wealth and good fortune. Houses are spring-cleaned, cards sent, new clothes and jewellery worn and food shared with family and friends. In the dark, windows glow with oil lamps or divas, and fireworks are let off.

In Britain, Leicester is one of the showpieces of Divali celebrations, and streets that have Indian shops and restaurants are decorated with fairy lights.

Background

The story behind the festival of Divali comes from one of the world's oldest epic poems the *Ramayana*. As in all the best epic stories, good overcomes evil.

Prince Rama and his wife Sita lived in a forest. One day Rama heard of a golden deer nearby and he took his bow and arrows to try to shoot it. While Rama was away a wicked demon with ten heads, called Ravana, snatched Sita away. As he flew with her back to his island of Lanka (now Sri Lanka), Sita took off her jewels and threw them to the ground. Ravana told Sita he would keep her prisoner until she agreed to be his wife.

Luckily Sugreeva, king of the monkeys, and Hanuman, his monkey army leader, found the jewels. As they wandered in the forest they met Rama searching for Sita.

Hanuman promised Rama he would find Sita. He followed the trail of jewels to Lanka and secretly told Sita she would be rescued.

Hanuman flew (a magic monkey, of course!) back to Rama and told him the news. Hanuman called together his monkey army and with Rama marched to the southern tip of India. The monkey army pulled down branches and rolled huge rocks to the edge of the sea and built a bridge to Lanka.

There was a great battle between Ravana, with his demons, and Rama, Hanuman and his army. Ravana had to be hit in the foot by one of Rama's arrows before he was killed.

Sita was rescued and she, Rama and Hanuman and his army crossed safely back to India, where everyone welcomed them home with little lamps or divas.

Divali drama

This story can be used for an exciting group drama. When using any story to create a play that encourages group participation, it is helpful to take a Pied Piper approach. The practitioner moves and tells the story, so if they wish all the children can take all the parts.

Resources

- The story in your head or on paper
- If possible, background music such as Indian sitar music by Ravi Shankar
- Construction bricks for a simple bridge
- A long piece of cloth or paper for the sea

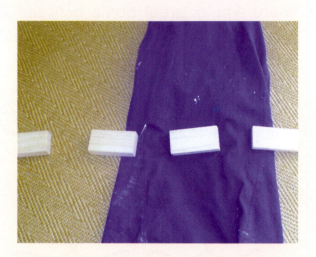

Aims/concepts

- To learn a little about one of the world's major literary works
- To begin to understand and enjoy a Sikh and Hindu festival
- To take part in imaginative role play
- To follow the sequence of a story
- To cooperate with others
- To gain confidence

Process

- Tell the story and something about the festival.
- Talk about how you can dramatise the story.
- Talk about the way monkeys will move and build a bridge.
- How can you 'play fight' without getting hurt?
- Tell the story, move as you do it, and let the children follow.

Discussion/language

Names of characters:

- Rama
- Sita
- Hanuman
- Ravana
- Demons
- Divas
- Lanka

Group size

Whole group

Links to Foundation Stage

CLL	SS	Use talk to connect ideas, explain what is happening and anticipate what might happen next.
	ELG	Use language to imagine and recreate roles and experiences.
KUW	SS	Gain an awareness of the cultures and beliefs of others.
	ELG	Begin to know about their own cultures and beliefs and those of other people.
CD	SS	Play cooperatively as part of a group to act out a narrative.
	ELG	Use their imagination in art and design, music and dance, imaginative and role play and stories.

Extension links

1. Look at a map or globe and find India and Sri Lanka.
2. Make a 'Rangoli pattern', p. 62. Either individually or as a group effort draw the shape and fill in by colouring or using lentils, rice, split peas, etc. glued on. Traditional Rangoli patterns are displayed in homes and temples.
3. Make coconut *barfi*. Indian sweets are popular gifts at Divali. See the photocopiable 'No cook coconut barfi', p. 63.
4. Make an instant Ravana; ten children stand in a line; count ten heads; stick out arms and count; stick out legs and count.
5. See Baisakhi (p. 15) for another Sikh festival and how to wear a sari, turban and shalwaar kameez.

Stories

- *The Amazing Adventures of Hanuman,* told by Rani and Jugnu Singh, illustrated by Biman Mullick, BBC Books, 1988.

Health and Safety

⚠ Take care with bridge-building or making stepping-stones.

⚠ Be careful not to bump into one another.

⚠ Remember play fighting!

Rangoli pattern

© Carolyn Hewitson (2004) *Festivals*, published by David Fulton Publishers Ltd.

No cook coconut barfi

Tin of condensed milk

Packet of desiccated coconut

Icing sugar

Mix ingredients together to form stiff dough. Either spread onto a tray, allow to set, and cut into squares; or roll into small balls. Sprinkle both shapes with a little icing sugar. Too much sugar can make a child cough or choke.

Remember any nut allergies.

© Carolyn Hewitson (2004) *Festivals*, published by David Fulton Publishers Ltd.

Introduction and background

Eid-ul-Fitr and Eid-ul-Adha are the only two festivals recognised by Islam.

Eid-ul-Fitr is the family festival at the end of Ramadan when daytime fasting ends. For three days there is special food, presents, cards, new clothes, visiting family and friends, giving to the poor and the spiritual awareness and happiness gained from fasting.

The Qur'an (Holy Book) explains Ramadan.

Help me not to indulge myself, O God;
Rather make me ready to deny myself some pleasures;
And, as I do so,
May I think of my responsibilities towards others, and feel myself
    nearer to you.

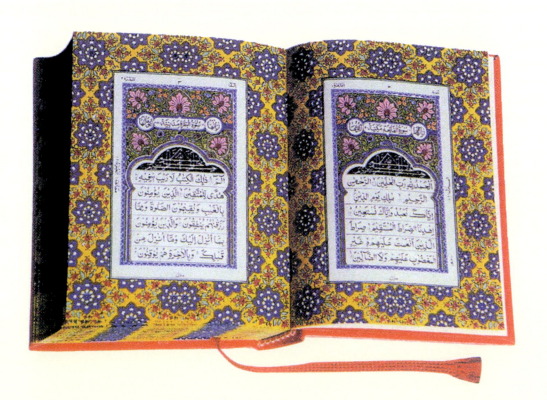

The Muslim calendar

Christians count their years from the year of Jesus' birth. Muslims count their years from the year the Holy Prophet Muhammad left Mecca and went to Medina on his journey known as the Hijra.

The calendar is based on the moon or 'lunar'. Each month begins when the new moon is seen. Their year is 354 days long, so this means that Muslim festivals move around the seasons.

There are Five Pillars of Islam:

1. Belief in one God, Allah, and in Muhammad his messenger.
2. Prayer, Namaz, to be performed five times a day.
3. Fasting for the month of Ramadan.
4. Charity, Zsakat.
5. Pilgrimage to Makkah, Hajj.

ACTIVITY 15

Make a garden

To learn something about being a Muslim and Islamic culture.

To make a garden or picture of a garden using an Islamic symmetrical shape.

Children to create gardens on their own or in groups.

To begin to understand the need for water for growth.

Resources

- Map or globe.
- Pictures of an Islamic garden and a Persian garden rug or a real rug.
- Steady tables, water, newspaper, paper roll.
- A model Islamic garden will need a square or rectangular dish or tray; damp soil or peat; aluminium foil for water; dried beans, lentils or tiny stones for gravel paths; twigs of small-leaved plants for shrubs and trees; any small pots or thumb pots made by children from clay or play dough, for planting with tiny twigs and positioning by the rills of aluminium foil.
- A child's garden will need a choice of plants and materials as well as any of the above. Suggestions are moss, stones, clumps of grass, small flowers or blossom.
- Understanding the need for water. This will need some quick-growing seeds such as mustard and cress or carrot tops grown with and without water. (These could be planted in your Islamic garden if you want it to last.)

Aims/concepts

- To begin to understand a little about being a Muslim and Islamic culture.
- To begin to know a little about geometric shape.
- To begin to understand the importance of gardens for fresh food, beauty and relaxation.
- To begin to understand the importance of water.
- To begin to know a little about history and the movement of cultures and ideas.

Process

- Show pictures of Islamic patterns, gardens and rugs.
- Show and eat fruits such as dates, apricots, almonds and pomegranates; if you want to eat a pomegranate eat the seeds, not the bitter pith. These are the fruits that you might find in an Islamic garden.

- Make a garden as a group with the above resources.
- Allow children, who wish, singly or in pairs, to make their own gardens.
- Plant mustard and cress on damp or dry soil or paper towel.
- Keep the damp soil or towel watered. Watch, predict and wait.

Discussion/language

- Talk about temples, churches, mosques, shrines, synagogues, etc. and familiarise children with the sound of these words.
- Do any of the children go to these places? Can they talk about it?
- Talk about a long time ago when people were nomads and wandered about looking for food and water and there were no towns. People wandered across deserts and found oases. Luckily some people found a wheat seed that they could grow and harvest to make into bread, so they settled there, built a town and after many years travelled, and built new towns, houses, mosques and gardens, usually in hot climates, so they needed shade and water. Show some of the fruits they brought with them (see 'Process').
- Garden shapes – square, rectangle, symmetric (a concept too difficult for most young children).
- Look at a map or globe and find where Arabic people created their first cities – look for Iraq, Iran, then travel through the Mediterranean to north Africa, Sicily, southern France and southern Spain.
- Talk about children's own gardens, what do they enjoy about them?
- What do they use them for?
- Why do we need water? How often do we use it every day?
- Where does it come from? How is it stored?

Links to Foundation Stage

PSED **SS** Talk freely about their home and community.

ELG Have a developing respect for their own cultures and those of other people.

MD **SS** Begin to use mathematical names... to describe shapes.

ELG Talk about, recognise and recreate simple patterns.

KUW **SS** Construct with a purpose in mind, using a variety of resources.

ELG Build and construct with a wide range of objects, selecting appropriate resources, and adapting their work where necessary.

CD **SS** Use one object to represent another, even when the objects have few characteristics in common.

ELG Use their imagination in art and design...

Group size

All together for initial discussion.
You may be able to plant your Islamic garden taking turns if the group is cooperative and small enough.
Four children for planting their own gardens.
All together for planting and observing carrot tops and cress.

Health and Safety

⚠ Hand-washing after handling soil.
⚠ Remember any allergies, especially if tasting nuts and fruit.
⚠ Is anything used poisonous?
⚠ Ensure small stones, lentils, etc. are not swallowed.

Extension links

Stories

- Tales from the *Arabian Nights*.

- Fruit in 'Oranges and Lemons', p. 21.
- Make an Islamic garden as a collage picture.
- This could be the beginning of a whole new topic about water!

- Make a Persian rug or carpet by dividing or folding a piece of material into four squares or rectangles; use the folds for the water rills and the quarters for planting. Use beads and sequins, turquoise, gold and silver to make patterns, as did the fabled carpet found in ancient Baghdad which was cut up and looted by invaders.
- Use equipment in your water play area to demonstrate how water flowing downhill can irrigate gardens, etc. and flowing with force make fountains – another feature of Islamic gardens.

History of Arab culture and civilisation

- The Holy Prophet Muhammad conquered Makkah or Mecca in AD 630, and by 730 the Muslim empire stretched from Spain and southern France to the borders of China and India.
- The Arabs spread their knowledge of mathematics and love of symmetry; as representation of the human body was usually prohibited to Muslims, they used geometric patterns, calligraphy and floral designs to decorate mosques and houses with tiles, mosaics, murals, carvings and hand woven carpets.
- Water is essential to all life, especially so to people who live surrounded by desert. Civilisation, meaning settled village or town life, began in the Middle East when nomads discovered they could tame a wild wheat seed, which by a happy genetic accident had crossed with another grass

to create the fertile emmer seed. Wheat could be grown and harvested and bread baked and nomads could fold away their tents, build their houses and tend their gardens. Water, usually at an oasis, was vital, and it was necessary to develop irrigation.

- Gardens with cooling water providing shade, reflection, beauty, time for meditation and relaxation became a metaphor for both an earthly and a heavenly paradise. 'Paradise' is derived from an ancient Persian word meaning enclosure or garden.
- This is a description of Paradise from the Qur'an:

> Blessed is the reward of those who labour patiently and put their trust in Allah [God]. Those that embrace the true faith and do good works shall be forever lodged in the mansions of Paradise, where rivers will roll at their feet . . . and honoured shall they be in the gardens of delight, upon couches face to face. A cup shall be borne round among them from a fountain limpid, delicious to those who drink. Their spouses on soft green cushions and on beautiful carpets shall recline.

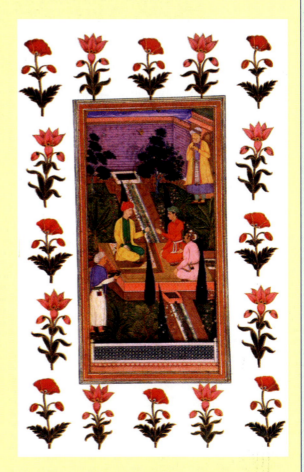

- The pattern of Islamic gardens is based on that of a Persian emperor Cyrus, who lived in 500 BC, and on a silk Persian carpet found at Ctesiphon (today's Baghdad), which represented a royal garden divided into four parts by rills and gravel paths, and planted with fruit trees in the geometrically shaped plots.
- One of the most easily accessible and beautiful Islamic gardens is the garden of the Alhambra and Generalife near Granada in southern Spain.
- Fruits such as pomegranates, oranges, lemons, peaches, apricots, almonds and date palms, and trees such as cypresses, would have been brought westwards by the spread of Islam.

16 Thanksgiving

Introduction and background

Thanksgiving is an American national holiday and is celebrated on the fourth Thursday of November. The first Thanksgiving was celebrated in November 1621 in the tiny colony of Plymouth, Massachusetts. In 1620 a group of Protestant dissenters, later called the Pilgrim Fathers, sailed from Plymouth, England, in the *Mayflower*. They hoped to find peace and freedom in America.

The Native American Indians helped them through the first winter, showing them how to grow pumpkins, squash, sweet potatoes and sweetcorn; how to catch cod and lobster, trap rabbits, venison, duck, goose and turkey, and pick cranberries; and how to tap maple trees for syrup. It was a time when settlers and Native Americans shared a peaceable kingdom very different from the later violence and genocide.

The Thanksgiving family meal's ingredients reflect the first Thanksgiving in Plymouth shared by settlers and Native Americans. Roast turkey, corn stuffing, cranberry sauce and pumpkin pie are the mainstays of the meal. It is a festival celebrated by all ethnic groups.

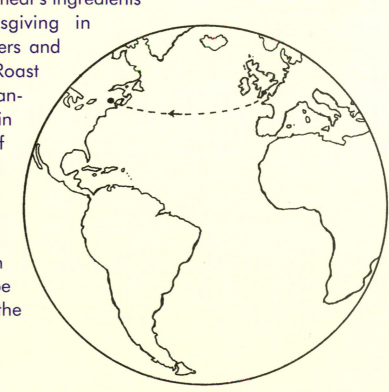

In 1863 President Lincoln decided that it should be celebrated throughout the USA.

ACTIVITY 16 Thanksgiving

To begin to learn a little about Thanksgiving and its origins. See the photocopiable 'Thanksgiving story', p. 76.

To listen to a poem, 'First Thanksgiving', photocopiable on p. 104.

To make a market stall or shop selling fruit and vegetables including especially those from America.

Resources

- The story about Thanksgiving (see p. 76)
- Poem about Thanksgiving (see p. 104)
- A play house, which can be made into a shop, or a table arrangement which can be a shop
- Scales
- Real or play money
- A variety of winter squashes and pumpkins
- Sweetcorn

(If you wish to emphasise fruit and vegetables to back up the Thanksgiving story, use the above. If you wish to use fruit and vegetables which originated in the Americas add tomatoes, peppers, blueberries, potatoes, avocado, beans – broad beans, runner beans, French beans, haricot beans, kidney beans and butter beans – and Jerusalem artichokes. If you want a general fruit and veg. shop, use your own selection of familiar and unfamiliar.)

- Baskets to display fruit and vegetables
- Bags for carrying them
- A till or containers for money
- Some children may want to play supermarkets, so you will need something as a pretend scanner
- Paper for receipts or tickets
- Pencils
- Name labels for fruit and vegetables
- Map or globe

Aims/concepts

- To find out about an American festival.
- To begin to know a little about history and migration of people and of fruit and veg!
- To begin to understand the concepts of money, counting and weighing.
- To play cooperatively.
- To learn more about fruit and vegetables.

Process

- Find America and Plymouth, UK on the globe or map.
- Tell the story of the Pilgrim Fathers and the Native Americans, see 'Thanksgiving story', p. 76.
- Read the poem 'First Thanksgiving', photocopiable on p. 104.
- Describe a Thanksgiving dinner; have some of the fruit and vegetables to examine, name and possibly taste. See the photocopiable 'Thanksgiving food', p. 105.
- Discuss and set up a stall or shop.
- Initiate play with groups of children.
- Let children play, observe and from time to time join in play and use the names of fruit and vegetables; help weigh, count and use money.
- Allow children to play as they wish with occasional adult input. Don't worry if they want to use it as a home corner.

Discussion/language

- Thanksgiving
- America
- Plymouth
- Colonists
- Indians (Columbus thought he had found a new route to India when he arrived in the Americas, and so he called the Native Americans Indians.)
- Puritans
- Pilgrim Fathers
- *Mayflower*
- How did they travel to America? What sort of ship did they sail in?
- Where would they live when they arrived? What sort of houses would they live in?
- How did they know what was safe and good to eat?
- Pumpkin
- Cranberries
- Squash
- Sweetcorn or Indian corn
- Succotash (a Native American Indian dish of sweetcorn and lima beans thickened with sunflower seed flour)
- Shops, markets, greengrocers, supermarkets, pick-your-own, grow-your-own – where do you get your fruit and vegetables?
- Could the Pilgrim Fathers and Native Americans go to shops? Sharing and exchanging
- Healthy eating – five a day
- How shall we set up our shop?
- What do we need?
- Scales, money, bags, fruit and vegetables
- Do we know where some of the fruit and vegetables come from? See 'Resources', p. 72.
- Names of some of the coins and weights
- Heavy, light, more, less
- Name the fruit and vegetables and use describing words – colour, shape, smell and texture
- Have children eaten them?

Group size

Whole group for introduction, background, story, poem and discussion.
Three to four for playing shop.

Extension links

1   More about vegetables – see 'Harvest', p. 57 with suggestions for tasting.
2   Oranges and Lemons fruit, see p. 21.
3   Pesach (Passover) fruit, see p. 32.
4   Lent – lemons, see p. 24.

Links to Foundation Stage

MD	SS	Order two items by weight...
	ELG	Use language such as 'greater', 'smaller', 'heavier' or 'lighter' to compare quantities.
KUW	SS	Begin to differentiate between past and present.
	ELG	Find out about past and present events...
PD	SS	Show some understanding that good practices with regard to...eating...can contribute to good health.
	ELG	Recognise the importance of keeping healthy and those things which contribute to this.
CD	SS	Engage in imaginative and role play based on own first-hand experiences.
	ELG	Use their imagination in...imaginative...role play.

Health and Safety

⚠ Allergies
⚠ Children have been known to swallow coins!

Thanksgiving story

The story of the first Thanksgiving

The Pilgrim Fathers came from a village called Scrooby in Nottinghamshire. They were Puritans who wanted simple church services and refused to go to Church of England worship. They settled in Holland, where there was freedom of worship. They could not find another group of Puritans whose views they agreed with, and their children were beginning to forget they were English, so they wanted to settle somewhere where they could be English and worship as they wished.

England owned a colony in America, and eventually on 6 September 1620 they sailed from Plymouth on the *Mayflower*. They landed in Cape Cod Bay in November. A party of men explored and found a suitable place for settling. On Christmas Day they began to build their first house. They were weak from their long journey and were ill with scurvy, a disease caused by lack of fruit and vegetables. By spring, half the colonists were dead.

They were befriended by Native Americans who showed them how to plant corn, squashes and pumpkins; how and what to hunt and fish; and where to pick cranberries and tap for maple syrup.

As the weather became warmer, life became better, 11 houses were built, and meat, fish, fruit, vegetables and flour made from ground corn used for bread-making could be stored for the winter. William Bradford the governor decided upon a Thanksgiving feast to thank God for their new life and successful harvest. They invited 90 Native Americans and their chief to their three-day feast.

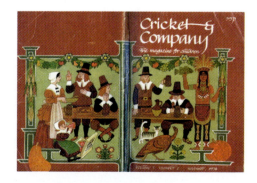

Can you see something the settlers or Native Americans could not have eaten?

© Carolyn Hewitson (2004) *Festivals*, published by David Fulton Publishers Ltd.

17 Saint Nicholas, Santa Claus and Father Christmas

Introduction and background

New Year has always been a time of gift-giving. The early Church used this much older tradition and made it one of giving in honour of baby Jesus. Different countries adopted different gift-bringers. In many countries of the world between 5 December and 6 January children receive gifts from a variety of imaginary benefactors. Spanish children receive their gifts from the Three Magi at Epiphany; Italian and Russian children receive them from elderly ladies, and in Scandinavia gnomes deliver the goodies.

The most widespread of gift-bringers is Father Christmas or Santa Claus. Both are based on Saint Nicholas, who was a bishop in Asia Minor, and died about AD 342. His remains are believed to be in the Basilica di San Nicola in Bari in south-east Italy, which became a place of pilgrimage. He became patron saint of Russia, and of children, merchants, sailors and those in danger.

A story is told that he threw a bag of gold down a chimney or in a window for three poor girls so they could get married. It landed in a stocking or a shoe. Whatever happened, several traditions were born. Saint Nicholas or Sinterklaas travelled to America with Dutch settlers, where the first church was dedicated to him in New Amsterdam, now New York. His name was anglicised into Santa Claus.

A poem by Dr Clement Clarke Moore, 'A visit from St Nicholas', was published in 1822 (see photocopiable p. 106) and St Nicholas became a cross between 'a jolly old elf' and the pagan character of Old Christmas found in English mummers' plays, and he turned into Father Christmas.

ACTIVITY 17 Dutch Christmas

To learn about and enjoy a Dutch Christmas tradition.

To estimate what will fit in a shoe.

Resources

- The background story
- Poem, 'A visit from St Nicholas', see photocopiable p. 106
- A shepherd's crook, walking stick, or something similar
- A red piece of cloth for a cloak, cotton wool twisted onto pipe cleaners or flexible wire, strong red card or paper and gold strip made into a bishop's mitre (see p. 77)

- A hobby horse or a piece of wood with a stuffed sock, buttons for eyes, pieces of card or felt for ears, attached to the wood. Alternatively have an imaginary horse and use coconuts for imaginary hooves.
- Everyone's shoes
- Hay or straw and carrots, a drink of water
- Little presents
- A stick

Aims/concepts

- To begin to learn about a tradition which Father Christmas is partly based on.
- Use developing mathematical ideas and methods to solve practical problems.

Process

- You the practitioner can dress up as Sinterklaas.
- Remember some children are frightened of a disguise which is too successful.
- Tell the children that Sinterklaas arrives by boat bringing his white horse and rides through the towns waving to and being greeted by them. On Saint Nicholas or Sinterklaas Eve, 5 December, children in Holland leave their shoes downstairs, one filled with carrots, one with hay or straw for the horse and a drink of water for Sinterklaas. If the children have been good there will be presents in the shoes; if they have been naughty, sticks will be left for a smack!
- When you have told the story, the children can take off their shoes, put carrots and hay in them and pretend to be asleep.
- Sinterklaas may need a drink of water.
- Leave little presents in the shoes and take away the hay, carrots and water.
- Let the children find a small toy in the room, which will fit into their shoes.
- Read the poem 'A visit from St Nicholas' (see photocopiable p. 106), or perhaps leave until later.

Group size

Story and poem – whole group

Discussion/language

- Father Christmas
- Saint Nicholas
- Sinterklaas
- Santa Claus
- Holland – where is it on a map or a globe?
- Bishop
- Mitre
- Crook for a shepherd to rescue his sheep, so for a bishop to rescue his flock or people (Jesus is called the Good Shepherd)
- Beard
- Cloak
- How do children in the class feel about Father Christmas and how do they prepare for him? N.B. Not all children celebrate Christmas or believe in Father Christmas.

Health and Safety

⚠ Take care with sticks.

Links to Foundation Stage

CLL	SS	Listen to stories with increasing attention and recall.
	ELG	Listen with enjoyment, and respond to stories ... and poems ...
MD	SS	Use size language such as big and little.
	ELG	Use developing mathematical ideas and methods to solve practical problems.
KUD	SS	Describe significant events for family or friends.
	ELG	Begin to know about their own cultures and beliefs and those of other people.

Extension links

- Christmas, p. 83.
- Stories about St. Nicholas or Father Christmas.
- *Father Christmas* by Raymond Briggs, published by Hamish Hamilton, 1973.
- *The Dutch Twins* by Lucy Fitch Perkins, published by Jonathan Cape, 1928, with many reprints.

Stories about Holland

- *Shadrach* by Meindert Dejong, published by William Collins Armada Lions, 1973.
- Making, baking and eating Speculaas Sinterklaas biscuits.
- Recipe, see 'Speculaas', p. 81.

Speculaas

Speculaas are spicy biscuits made specially for the Dutch Sinterklaas festival.

They are traditionally made using a mould shown opposite, but these are very difficult to use because the dough must be removed very carefully with a sharp knife. I suggest you invest in some Christmas biscuit cutters. Take care they are not too sharp.

Speculaas recipe

I use a gingerbread man dough which is very similar to the original Speculaas recipe and will put up with much handling and rolling.

Makes about 25–30 depending on the size of the cutters.

75g soft brown sugar, with lumps sieved out

1 tablespoon water

3 tablespoons golden syrup

95g butter

1 teaspoon ginger

1 teaspoon cinnamon

Grated rind of an orange

225g plain flour

Half a teaspoon bicarbonate of soda

The ingredients can be prepared with help from the children.

The next stage should be watched by the children from a safe distance.

Bring the sugar, syrup, water, spices and orange rind to the boil in a pan; stir all the time.

Remove from the heat and stir in the butter and bicarbonate of soda.

Follow with the flour a spoon at a time. It needs to be like a smooth play dough so you may need a little more flour.

Let the dough cool in a plastic bag in the fridge for about 30 minutes.

Quarter the dough and roll out the pieces to about 3mm thick. Cut out and place on a greased tin.

Bake in the oven, gas mark 4, 350 °F, 180 °C for 10–15 minutes. They should feel firm when you press them lightly. Let them cool in the tin. If you wish to decorate the biscuits place chocolate buttons when the biscuit is still warm. Sieve a little icing sugar to scatter; too much can make children cough and choke.

© Carolyn Hewitson (2004) *Festivals*, published by David Fulton Publishers Ltd.

Christmas

Introduction and background

Christians celebrate 25 December as the birthday of Jesus. Unique celebrations of Christmas by different cultures throughout the world have tended to be lost and the real meaning of these Christmas rituals, some pre-Christian, can only be guessed at. The pre-Christian festivals of Roman Saturnalia and Viking Yuletide brought light into the winter darkness at the time when the sun appears to be reborn after the winter solstice. These old pre-Christian customs were adapted to the new Christian religion, and although our modern Christmas is very much a Victorian invention, many pagan practices remain.

Many pre-Christian societies encouraged and celebrated the return of the sun by bringing in evergreens that were symbols of continuing life in the darkest days of winter. In some parts of Europe branches and small trees were brought inside to try to make them blossom at Christmas. We still follow this custom when we force hyacinth bulbs or buy hothouse plants. The poinsettia, which is popular all over the world, comes from a Mexican story. A small boy, who had nothing to place by the *posada* or nativity scene, found a beautiful red-leafed plant growing where he had knelt. It is said to resemble the star of Bethlehem. The Mexicans call it the flower of the Holy Night, but usually it is called poinsettia after the man who introduced it to America, Dr Joel Poinsett.

Although greenery has been brought into the house since pre-Christian times, the Christmas tree is a relative newcomer. For many people it is one of the true symbols of the Christmas season. It is evergreen, decorated with light to symbolise the return of the sun and regrowth, and links with present giving and family gatherings. Christmas trees became popular in Britain after 1840 when Prince Albert introduced this German custom to his wife Queen Victoria and their children, and so to the country. It is known that Christmas fir trees were already well established in Alsace by 1605, when they were described being hung with roses made of many-coloured paper, apples, wafers, gold foil and sweets.

ACTIVITY 18 Christmas trees

To learn something about the traditions of Christmas.

To learn about trees and leaves.

To make simple, meaningful decorations for a Christmas tree or branch.

To listen to a traditional German story.

To cooperate with others making decorations and anticipate, for most children, the happy family time of Christmas.

N.B. Some children do not celebrate Christmas. Jehovah's Witnesses do not, and some parents of children of non-Christian faiths may be happier with the secular side of Christmas; you must find out.

Resources

- An assortment of fallen leaves, e.g. oak, beech, sycamore.
- Pine cones, acorns, old man's beard, or hips and haws, anything suitable found on a walk through trees in a park, around a garden, a wood or an arboretum.
- Small gourds, nuts in their shells or fruit could be added.
- A Christmas tree, with roots if possible, or an evergreen branch.
- Something steady and safe to stand it on.
- A steady table covered with newspaper.
- Aprons.
- Gold or silver paint.
- Paintbrushes.
- The fir tree story, see 'The fir tree', photocopiable p. 87.
- Pictures or, if possible, leaves from a palm tree, an olive tree and a fir tree.

Aims/concepts

- To begin to understand the difference between deciduous and evergreen trees.
- To begin to understand something about the traditions of Christmas.
- To cooperate together to make their own decorations.

Process

- Collect leaves, cones, etc. on a walk or outing. Many local parks, forests and woods have nature trails and teachers' centres. Try the Forestry Commission in the Yellow Pages or on the Internet.
- Look at the deciduous trees which have lost their leaves and the evergreens. Perhaps you and the children can name some of the trees.
- Perhaps you can buy your Christmas tree on your outing.
- Enjoy the trees; walk under and around them, lie down and look up at them.
- When you are ready, paint your leaves, etc. with gold and/or silver paint. No need to cover them with paint, touches here and there will do.
- Decorate your tree. You could make holes in the leaves, etc. but I think leaves scattered on and a few drifting below the tree look very effective.
- Tell the fir tree story, see p. 87.

Group Size

All together for tree outing, discussion, story and tree decoration.
Four to six children for leaf, cone, etc. painting.

Links to Foundation Stage

KUW SS Examine objects and living things to find out more about them.

ELG Find out about and identify some features of living things, objects and events they observe.

CD SS Choose particular colours to use for a purpose.

ELG Explore colour, texture, shape, form and space in two or three dimensions.

Health and Safety

- ⚠ You have guidelines for outings.
- ⚠ Berries can be poisonous.
- ⚠ Take care with gold and silver paint.

Discussion/language

- Look out of the window and talk about any trees you can see.
- Tall, shady, colour, deciduous or evergreen, what is it called? (You may need a book about trees.)
- Look around the room. What is made of wood?
- What else do we use wood for?
- Paper, a fire to keep us warm, sports equipment, musical instruments, etc.
- Parts of a tree – roots, trunks, branches, twigs, bark.
- Leaves, veins.
- Who lives in a tree? – birds, squirrels, insects.
- Compare leaf shape and size, look at pine needles.
- What happens to leaves when they fall? What do worms do to them?
- Compost, soil.
- Fir trees, their shape, evergreen, cones.
- How do the children decorate their trees?
- Are they real trees with roots?
- Talk about bringing greenery into the house and using fairy lights in the dark days of winter.
- Tell the fir tree story.

Extension links

Saint Nicholas, p. 77.

Stories about trees

The Giving Tree, by Shel Silverstein, tells the story of a tree and a boy growing older together.

Leaf printing

See fruit and vegetable printing, 'Harvest', p. 54.

Leaf rubbing

Place a leaf vein side up, put paper on top, use a thick wax crayon on its side and crayon over until the leaf can be seen on the paper.

- Make a Christmas tree print by using a piece of wood with string glued on in a Christmas tree shape and print using paint mixture as used in 'Harvest', p. 54. See illustration above. Use the handle end of a paintbrush to make little blobs of gold or silver paint for candles or fairy lights.
- Try growing an acorn or conker.
- Look at the rings on a tree stump or a log. Can you count the rings and tell the age of the tree?

The fir tree

A traditional German story

When Jesus was born in a stable, three trees grew outside. There was a palm tree, an olive tree and a fir tree. As the trees watched the shepherds and kings bringing gifts for the baby, they wanted to bring their own presents.

The palm said, 'I will give him my largest leaf and his mother Mary can use it as a fan.'

The olive said, 'I will give my oil, so his mother Mary can use it to make his skin soft and sweet-smelling.'

The fir said, 'What can I give?'

'You have nothing to give, only prickly needles, which would scratch the baby's soft skin.' Said the palm and the olive.

The fir tree felt very sad and wished it had something to give, but it wasn't jealous of the two other trees. An angel was watching and listening to the trees. The angel took pity on the kind little tree and called to the tiny, twinkling stars in the dark sky to come down and rest in the branches of the fir tree.

The little fir tree glowed in the darkness and the baby laughed and clapped his tiny hands. That is why we remember him with a fir tree decorated with candles or lights.

© Carolyn Hewitson (2004) *Festivals*, published by David Fulton Publishers Ltd.

Photocopiable materials

January brings the snow

January brings the snow,
Makes our feet and fingers glow.
February brings the rain,
Melts the frozen pond again.
March brings winds to blow your kite,
And rattle windows in the night.
April has both sun and showers,
To wet your feet and grow the flowers.
May is the month of new green leaves,
When birds are nestling under the eaves.
June contains the longest day,
With hours of sun for all your play.
Although July is very warm,
It sometimes brings a thunderstorm.
August is full of hot dry days,
Sea and sand and holidays.
September brings a cooler breeze,
And fruit and nuts upon the trees.
October turns the leaves to brown,
And chilly winds to blow them down.
Dull November dark and nippy,
Making roads and pavements slippy.
Cold December brings the sleet,
And presents for your Christmas treat.

© Carolyn Hewitson (2004) *Festivals*, published by David Fulton Publishers Ltd.

Chinese New Year calendar

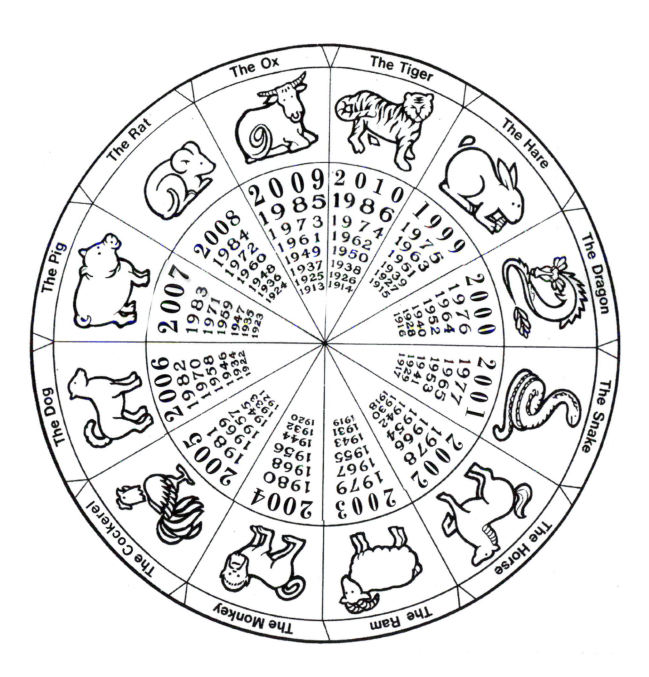

© Carolyn Hewitson (2004) *Festivals*, published by David Fulton Publishers Ltd.

Animals

© Carolyn Hewitson (2004) *Festivals*, published by David Fulton Publishers Ltd.

Chapter 3 – No Ruz ('Process', p. 12): photocopiable

Goldfish

© Carolyn Hewitson (2004) *Festivals*, published by David Fulton Publishers Ltd.

How to put on a sari

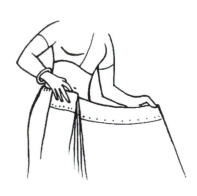

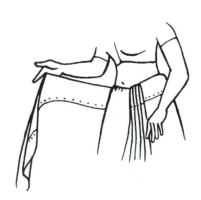

© Carolyn Hewitson (2004) *Festivals*, published by David Fulton Publishers Ltd.

How to put on a turban

© Carolyn Hewitson (2004) *Festivals*, published by David Fulton Publishers Ltd.

A picture of a shalwaar kameez

© Carolyn Hewitson (2004) *Festivals*, published by David Fulton Publishers Ltd.

Oranges and Lemons nursery rhyme

Oranges and Lemons

'Oranges and Lemons,'

said the bells of St Clements.

'You owe me five farthings,'

said the bells of St Martin's.

'When will you pay me?'

said the bells of Old Bailey.

'When I grow rich,'

said the bells of Shoreditch.

'Pray, when will that be?'

said the bells of Stepney.

'I'm sure I don't know,'

said the great bell of Bow.

Here comes a candle to light you to bed,

Here comes a chopper to chop off your head.

Chip-Chop-Chip-Chop,

The last man is dead.

© Carolyn Hewitson (2004) *Festivals*, published by David Fulton Publishers Ltd.

Orange and Lemon biscuit recipe

125g self-raising flour

60g caster sugar

75g butter

Grated rind and juice of 1 orange or lemon

Rub flour, sugar and butter together.

When the mixture is like breadcrumbs, add rind and enough juice to make a smooth dough.

Roll out to 5mm thickness.

Cut with biscuit shaper.

Place on greased baking sheet.

Place in oven at 350 °F (180 °C) (gas mark 4) for 10–15 minutes until just turning golden brown.

Remove from oven and allow to cool.

© Carolyn Hewitson (2004) *Festivals*, published by David Fulton Publishers Ltd.

Pancake poem

Mix a pancake,

Stir a pancake,

Pop it in the pan,

Fry the pancake,

Toss the pancake,

Catch it if you can.

Christina Rossetti

© Carolyn Hewitson (2004) *Festivals*, published by David Fulton Publishers Ltd.

Charoset recipe

For eight children

One large apple grated or chopped
200g walnuts chopped (N.B. nut allergies)
Six teaspoons each of sugar and cinnamon,
perhaps less cinnamon according to taste.
Enough grape juice to make a mortar-like
consistency.

The chopping will probably be best done by an
adult, the mixing and sharing out by the children.

Other symbolic foods eaten at the Seder table are

1. A roasted lamb shank bone
2. A roasted egg
3. A root of horseradish
4. A dish of salt water
5. A sprig of bitter herbs

© Carolyn Hewitson (2004) *Festivals*, published by David Fulton Publishers Ltd.

The doll festival*

Lighted lanterns
cast a gentle radiance
on pink peach blossoms.

Third day of third month.
Mother brings out five long shelves --
black lacquer, red silk.

On the topmost shelf
we place gilded folding screens
and the two chief dolls.

They are Emperor
and Empress, in formal robes:
gauzes, silks, brocades.

On the lower steps,
court ladies with banquet trays,
samisen players.

Should the royal pair
wish to go blossom-viewing –
two golden palanquins.

High officials, too,
kneeling in solemn stillness:
young noble pages.

Third day of third month.
Our small house holds a palace –
we are its guardians.

Fairy furniture –
dressers, mirrors, lacquer bowls,
bonsai, fans, braziers.

Lighted lanterns
cast a gentle radiance
on pink peach blossoms.

James Kirkup

**Long ago, the Japanese used dolls to drive away evil spirits.
On March 3rd, Japanese children celebrate the Doll festival by
creating a royal court, consisting of a set of 15 dolls on stands
draped with red cloth.*

© Carolyn Hewitson (2004) *Festivals*, published by David Fulton Publishers Ltd.

Elephant template

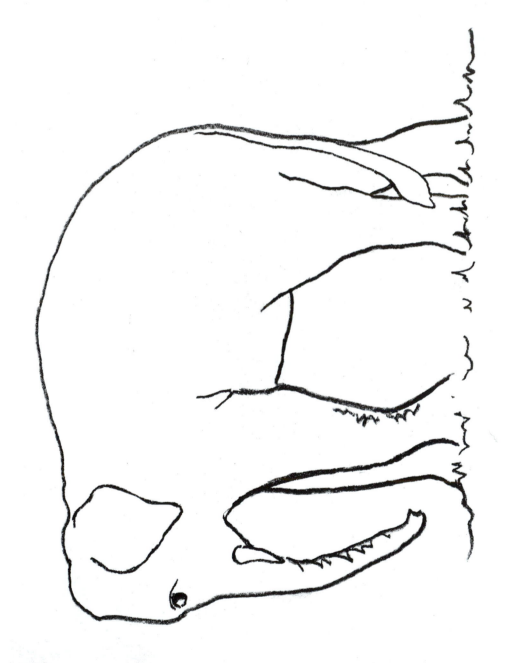

© Carolyn Hewitson (2004) *Festivals*, published by David Fulton Publishers Ltd.

Chapter 11 – Japanese Boys' Day or Children's Day ('Resources', p. 44): photocopiable

Carp template

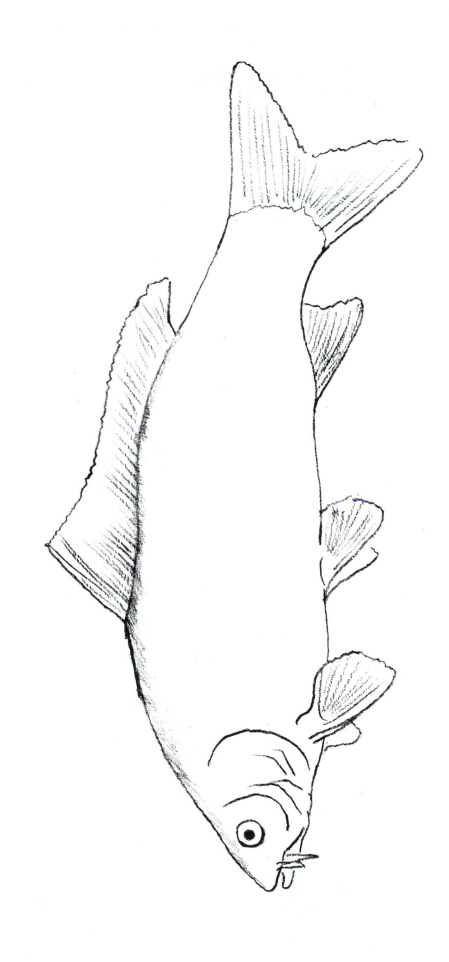

© Carolyn Hewitson (2004) *Festivals*, published by David Fulton Publishers Ltd.

First Thanksgiving

FIRST
THANKSGIVING

Myra Cohn Livingston

Three days we had,
 feasting, praying, singing.

Three days outdoors at wooden tables,
Colonists and Indians together,
Celebrating a full harvest,
A golden summer of corn.

   We hunted the woods, finding
   Venison, deer, and wild turkey.

   We brought our plump geese and ducks,
   Great catches of silver fish.

   We baked corn meal bread with nuts,
   Journey cake, and steaming succotash.

   We roasted the meat on spits
   Before huge, leaping fires.

   We stewed our tawny pumpkins
   In buckets of bubbling maple sap.

Three days we had,
 feasting, praying, singing.

Three days outdoors at wooden tables,
Colonists and Indians together,
Celebrating a full harvest,
Praying, each to our God.

copyright © 1975 by Myra Cohn Livingston

© Carolyn Hewitson (2004) *Festivals*, published by David Fulton Publishers Ltd.

Thanksgiving food

Sweetcorn or maize is dried and ground into flour, which can be made into corn bread.

Use easy cook Italian polenta flour, which is the same, to make a soft polenta, cut into triangles when cold and fry in a little oil.

Pumpkins and squashes

To make pumpkin purée, take a wedge of pumpkin, winter squash or butternut squash, remove seeds and fibres, place on an oiled tray, cover with foil and bake in a medium oven until soft. When cool, scoop out pulp, and mash or process. Put in a sieve lined with muslin or a clean cotton hankie and leave overnight to drain.

Warm in a pan with a little cinnamon and ginger and maple syrup to sweeten.

The Pilgrim Fathers did not have cows, so no milk, cream or butter. They didn't have wheat, so no pastry pumpkin pies could be made.

Turkey

There is mention of boiled turkey, although the settlers referred to any type of partridge-like bird as turkey, but I think turkey breast is allowed (whole roast turkey is usually served at modern Thanksgiving dinners). It would be delicious with the polenta and some cranberry sauce.

© Carolyn Hewitson (2004) *Festivals*, published by David Fulton Publishers Ltd.

A visit from St Nicholas

A Visit from St Nicholas

CLEMENT C. MOORE

'Twas the night before Christmas, when all through the house
Not a creature was stirring, not even a mouse;
The stockings were hung by the chimney with care,
In hopes that St Nicholas soon would be there;
The children were nestled all snug in their beds,
While visions of sugar-plums danced in their heads;
And Mamma in her kerchief, and I in my cap,
Had just settled our brains for a long winter's nap,
When out on the lawn there arose such a clatter,
I sprang from the bed to see what was the matter.
Away to the window I flew like a flash,
Tore open the shutters and threw up the sash.
The moon on the breast of the new-fallen snow
Gave the lustre of midday to objects below,
When, what to my wondering eyes should appear,
But a miniature sleigh, and eight tiny reindeer,
With a little old driver, so lively and quick,
I knew in a moment it must be St Nick.
More rapid than eagles his coursers they came,
And he whistled, and shouted, and called them by name:
Now, Dasher! now Dancer! now Prancer and Vixen!
On, Comet! on, Cupid! on, Donner and Blitzen!
To the top of the porch! to the top of the wall!
Now dash away! dash away! dash away all!'
As dry leaves that before the wild hurricane fly,
When they meet with an obstacle, mount to the sky.
So up to the house-top the coursers they flew,
With the sleigh full of toys, and St Nicholas too.

And then, in a twinkling, I heard on the roof
The prancing and pawing of each little hoof.
As I drew in my head, and was turning around,
Down the chimney St Nicholas came with a bound.
He was dressed all in fur, from his head to his foot,
And his clothes were all tarnished with ashes and soot;
A bundle of toys he had flung on his back,
And he looked like a pedlar just opening his pack.
His eyes – how they twinkled! his dimples how merry!
His cheeks were like roses, his nose like a cherry!
His droll little mouth was drawn up like a bow,
And the beard of his chin was as white as the snow;
The stump of a pipe he held tight in his teeth,
And the smoke it encircled his head like a wreath;
He had a broad face and a little round belly,
That shook when he laughed, like a bowlful of jelly.
He was chubby and plump, a right jolly old elf,
And I laughed when I saw him, in spite of myself;
A wink of his eye and a twist of his head
Soon gave me to know I had nothing to dread.
He spoke not a word, but went straight to his work,
And filled all the stockings; then turned with a jerk,
And laying his finger aside of his nose,
And giving a nod, up the chimney he rose;
He sprang to his sleigh, to his team gave a whistle,
And away they all flew like the down of a thistle.
But I heard him exclaim, ere he drove out of sight,
Happy Christmas to all and to all a good night.

© Carolyn Hewitson (2004) *Festivals*, published by David Fulton Publishers Ltd.

Bibliography

John Agard and Grace Nichols, (eds) *A Caribbean Dozen*, Walker Books, 1996.

Edward and Aingelda Ardizzone, *The Little Girl and the Tiny Doll*, A Young Puffin, 1979.

John and Gillian Beer, *Delights and Warnings: A New Anthology of Poems*, Macdonald, 1984.

Stan and Jan Berenstain, *Old Hat, New Hat*, Collins Picture Lions, 1973.

Raymond Briggs, *Father Christmas*, Hamish Hamilton, 1973.

John Burningham, *Avocado Baby*, Jonathan Cape, 1982.

Eric Carle, *The Very Hungry Caterpillar*, Hamish Hamilton, 1970.

Meindert Dejong, *Shadrach*, William Collins Armada Lions, 1973.

P. D. Eastman, *Flap Your Wings*, Collins Early Bird series, 1969.

Sue Fitzjohn, Minda Weston and Judy Large, *Festivals Together: A Guide to Multi-Cultural Celebration*, Hawthorn Press, 1993; reprinted 2003.

Marjorie Flack and Kurt Wiese, *The Story about Ping*, Bodley Head, 1935; now in its 16th impression.

Margaret Greaves, *Once There Were No Pandas: A Chinese Legend*, illustrated by Beverley Gooding, Methuen, 1985.

Gail Haley, *A Story, A Story*, Methuen Children's Books, 1972.

Barnabas and Anabel Kindersley, *Celebration*, Children Just Like Me series, Dorling Kindersley, 1997.

Rudyard Kipling, *Just So Stories*, Macmillan, 1902.

Jennie Lindon, *Understanding World Religions in Early Years Practice*, Hodder & Stoughton, 1999.

David McKee, *Elmer: The Story of a Patchwork Elephant*, Dobson, 1968.

Doris Orgel, *Sarah's Room*, illustrated by Maurice Sendak, Bodley Head, 1972.

Lucy Fitch Perkins, *The Dutch Twins*, Jonathan Cape, 1928.

John Godfrey Saxe, *The Blind Men and the Elephant*, illustrated by Paul Galdone, World's Work, 1964.

Maurice Sendak, *Chicken Soup with Rice: A Book of Months*, Collins, 1964; sixth impression 1988.

Shel Silverstein, *The Giving Tree*, Harper & Row, 1964.

Rani and Jugnu Singh, *The Amazing Adventures of Hanuman*, illustrated by Biman Mullick, BBC Books, 1988.

Jessica Souhami, *The Leopard's Drum*, Frances Lincoln, 1995.

Elfrida Vipont, *The Elephant and the Bad Baby*, illustrated by Raymond Briggs, Picture Puffin, 1971.

Shigeo Watanabe, *How Do I Put It On?*, Bodley Head, 1979.

Harve Zemach, *Buy Me a China Doll*, Blackie, 1969.

Charlotte Zolotow, *Mr Rabbit and the Lovely Present*, illustrated by Maurice Sendak, HarperCollins Picture Lions, 1992.

7057